Battleground Europe

RIQUEVAL

Battleground Europe

RIQUEVAL

K W Mitchinson

Series editor
Nigel Cave

LEO COOPER

First published in 1998 by
LEO COOPER
an imprint of
Pen Sword Books Limited
47 Church Street, Barnsley, South Yorkshire S70 2AS

Copyright © K W Mitchinson

ISBN 0 85052 622 1

A CIP catalogue of this book is available
from the British Library

Printed by Redwood Books Limited
Trowbridge, Wiltshire

For up-to-date information on other titles produced under the Leo Cooper imprint,
please telephone or write to:
Pen & Sword Books Ltd, FREEPOST, 47 Church Street
Barnsley, South Yorkshire S70 2AS
Telephone 01226 734222

CONTENTS

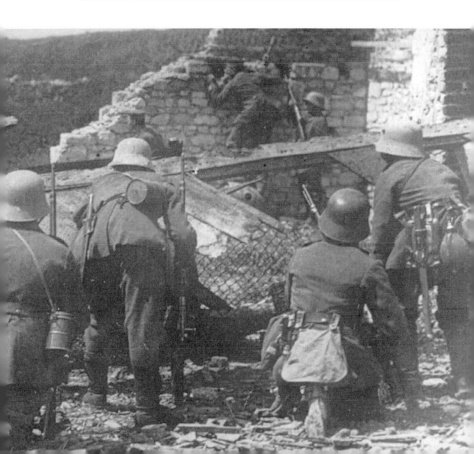

INTRODUCTION BY
SERIES EDITOR

This is the first in what will be a series of Battleground Europe books on a much neglected part of the battlefields of the Great War. This is largely a consequence of the fact that there is less obvious physical sign of the fighting as there is, say, on the Somme and in the Salient. The fighting here was over a shorter period of time and the battles – particularly those of the German spring offensive and the Advance to Victory in 1918 – moved quickly over the ground.

Yet it is a mistake not to take as much notice of the battles here as is paid to the slogging fights around the Somme, Arras, French Flanders and the Ypres Salient. Here the developments of tactics by both sides reached their peak – the German defensive systems along the Hindenburg Line, the attempt by the Fifth Army to create a new defensive system of their own for the inevitable German attack in 1918, the strategy and tactics of the German storm troopers in their seemingly unstoppable attempt to put a breach between the French and British armies and, finally, the massive use of artillery, air supremacy, tanks (where available), cavalry and infantry by the British, Dominion and American forces as they swept all before them on their advance to the Rhine.

Bill Mitchinson has chosen Riqueval as the first area along this vital front to be examined. It is a place perhaps most renowned for the heroic crossing of the St Quentin Canal by the 46th (North Midland) Division. For these men it was a welcome opportunity to bury the grim memories of the disaster at Gommecourt on the First Day of the Somme.

Although the tours are of a slightly different nature to others in the series, they continue in the tradition of explaining the events on the battlefield in the context of the ground. This is an essential (though often overlooked) element in understanding what happened here and why. We can state with certainty that the events of September 1918 rank amongst the greatest achievements of the British Army in its entire history – and are probably the least acknowledged.

Nigel Cave Ely Place London

The area covered by this b is inside the white lines.

— **Staring Line** • • • • **Main Hindenburg Line**
ACK ON HINDENBURG LINE, 18 SEPT 1918

INTRODUCTION

Although the photograph of the Staffordshire Brigade sitting on the canal bank at Riqueval is one of the most evocative and well-known of the war, few British tourists visit the hamlet and the surrounding villages. Those that do normally walk across the bridge, gaze in wonder at the steepness of the embankment and then drive north to the US memorial. Although largely unrecognised, Riqueval as an area has much to offer the inquisitive and knowledgeable visitor.

The construction of the motorway in the 1980s has added an air of modernity to an otherwise ancient and working landscape. Villages, regrown from the mounds of razed rubble which littered the region in 1917, are generally small; their fields are criss-crossed by grass baulks and are unfenced. Few of the tracks and woods are *Privé* and there is little traffic on the network of small roads. Some of the scenery, especially that in the Omignon Valley, is beautiful, and there is an abundance of active and colourful wildlife. There are also British cemeteries and, of course, your imagination.

A sign proudly erected by the Territorials of the 8/Warwick, 48th Division, in front of Péronne church. The rebuilt church now has a statue to the town's 16th century heroine, Marie Fouré, on almost the same site.

The squat bulk of St Quentin's basilica dominates the country for miles around. Badly damaged during the final year of the war, here it is shown in its early stages of reconstruction. TAYLOR LIBRARY

British troops pushed their way into the devastated zone in March 1917. German destruction of the villages and woods made it a painful and slow advance. The closer the British drew to the prepared defences of the Hindenburg Line, the fiercer became the opposition. Amid the snow, gales and then heat of 1917, the British attempted to gain ascendancy over the land in front of the German outpost line. Although lacking the intensity and duration of the battles further north, the fighting was bitter and bloody. In March 1918 the German onslaught fell upon Fifth Army; the Omignon Valley, and the higher ground either side, became a crucial objective to both defenders and attackers. Villages such as Le Verguier, Vadencourt and Hesbécourt, now scenes of rural tranquillity, witnessed violence on an unprecedented scale. Once again in September 1918, their pummelled ruins became the stage for yet more blood-letting. Little remains to remind the visitor of this belligerence today except the cemeteries. There are a few concrete bunkers and occasional vestiges of trenches, but the fields are again swollen with crops and the woods the home of deer and birds. Peace soon returned to this troubled part of France.

The area is easily and quickly reached from Péronne and St Quentin. Even the more traditional haunts of British visitors, Albert and its surrounding villages, are only 40 minutes away by car. It is for this reason that no list of available accommodation is provided in this book. Regular travellers to the Somme have their own preferred billet, so use that. It is ideal ground for walking and cycling, and it is for these tourists that this and its companion books on Epéhy and Villers-Plouich are primarily targeted. Use your common sense and what powers of the French language you possess to explore the miles of headlands and baulks. Keep to these, avoid the crops and no-one will bother you other than to wish you 'Bonjour'.

ACKNOWLEDGEMENTS

The information contained within these pages comes from many years of walking and cycling the area, and from a variety of primary and secondary sources. War diaries of the units which fought in the village and its surrounds have been used as the principal source of primary information. The detail found within those records has been supplemented by that taken from divisional, regimental and battalion histories and from personal reminiscences.

As it is not intended to be an academic book, I have followed the tradition now established in the Battleground series not to fully reference all information. Only the sources of direct quotations are given in the notes which follow each chapter. The bibliography lists many of the more easily accessible books consulted for the work. Several city reference libraries hold some of these volumes, but the serious reader is advised to visit the Imperial War Museum's Department of Printed Books. In order to save space, the several dozen war diaries (and their PRO reference numbers) which were used have not been included in the bibliography.

I extend my grateful thanks to the staffs of the Public Record Office and the IWM's Departments of Photographs and Printed Books. Mary Bayliss and her colleagues have, as usual, been of immense help and encouragement. The Trustees of both archives have granted permission to use material taken from their collections. My thanks also to the ladies of Accrington Library. Their collection of Commonwealth War Graves Commission registers has been of great use and their kindness has been much appreciated. Several individuals, in particular Nigel Cave, Kevin Kelly, David Key and Peter Oldham, have given of their expertise and made constructive criticism. I also offer thanks to the many French farmers and labourers who over the years have shown such tolerance at my less than adequate French. Their patience in attempting to understand my malapropisms has been appreciated.

Finally, special thanks to JB, my walking companion of many years. Her company and constant interest in my obsession with ploughed fields and tangled copses has made the trips so much more rewarding.

GENERAL ADVICE

As the area and its history is not as well known as most sectors of the British zones on the Western Front, there is rather more detail on the events than in other books of the same series. Each chapter is self-contained, with a military history of the area, a description of the area today, a map and a suggested walking or cycling tour. Figures in bold print in the text refer to points of interest marked on the map. It is suggested that the reader should familiarise his or herself with the military detail and the general lie of the land during the long winter nights preceding the next expedition. Cemeteries are arranged alphabetically at the rear of the book. The list includes details of those cemeteries which can be passed or reached by a short diversion while on the way to the region covered by the book. The size of the book is designed to fit easily into a pocket. Take it with you when you go but, for purposes of greater appreciation and continuity, try to have committed the position and principal characteristics of the sites to memory. An initial tour of the villages by car will help the visitor to understand the topography and relative distances.

Early spring and late autumn are the best times for visiting the Western Front. With the crops either low or gone completely, there is little to obscure the physical remains and the land itself. Another great advantage is the absence of nettles. Do not try to walk or bike most of the routes in summer wearing shorts. There is the occasional dock leaf,

The jumbled wreckage of Roisel in July 1917. This important railway junction was evacuated by the Germans in March 1917 and by British units on 22-23 March 1918.

but never in the right place. Wear sensible shoes, take a waterproof, sun cream, a compass and some liquid and solid sustenance. There are cafés about, but do not rely upon them. Visit a supermarket or *boulangerie* in Albert or Péronne before you set off. A stick is useful for poking about in the banks and undergrowth. If on a bike, take the usual spare inner tube, levers, basic spanners and pump. The terrain is easy for any experienced mountain biker: the climbs gentle, few rock steps and not many roots. Mud and tractor ruts can add to otherwise fairly mundane rides. Take the usual precautions against tetanus and carry your E111.

Park your car in an appropriate place. Remember, it is an offence to park on the side of a road; the car must be completely off the tarmac. Neither should you park on the exit of a headland. There might not be a tractor in sight when you leave the vehicle, but one will inevitably arrive as soon as you have left. Thoughtless actions like this do nothing to foster the *entente cordiale*. Neither should you, of course, wander about with a metal detector, dig holes in farmers' fields or collect ordnance. Finally, if walking the fields in autumn or winter, beware of weekend 'hunters'. They are a considerable menace and perfectly capable of loosing off a couple of rounds at a bird flying perilously close to your head. These men, who are usually commuters rather than farmers, need to be watched carefully.

MAPS

Most British tourists to the Somme carry the Michelin 1:200000 No.53 as their essential companion. The same map also covers the area around Riqueval. This map is perfectly adequate for the driver and casual wanderer. The IGN series of 1:25000 gives a much more detailed coverage, but for the really interested walker or cyclist, the 1:10000 trench maps are essential. These maps can be purchased from the IWM's Department of Printed Books and the Western Front Association. A pedometer or mileometer is a useful addition to your equipment.

This volume includes extracts from some of the official trench maps and hand drawn 'tour maps'. These latter maps vary in scale but have the same symbols. Modern road numbers and cemeteries have been included in order to aid orientation. Village and place names are spelt in the manner used by the army in 1917 and 1918. This does, however, cause one or two anomalies. For example, the hamlet now known as Vadancourt was spelt as Vadencourt by the British.[1]

Gillemont Farm was sometimes written as Guillemont, but the former spelling has been used throughout. Dotted lines indicate tracks and paths which, as a general rule, should not be driven. At some times of the year, several of them are passable, but you will not endear yourself to the tractor driver coming in the opposite direction. Many of those shown are grass baulks rather than tracks. The vegetation can hide discarded wire and other dangers. Efforts to find a level, firm spot to jack up the car and change a wheel can be rather difficult.

The 'tour maps' give an indication of the distance and an idea of the time needed to walk the route. If they seem a little ambitious, they can easily be shortened or amended. Walking and lingering in the area is a very rewarding experience. There is much to attract the eye and interest. Just use your common sense and knowledge to enjoy its delights.

1. There is a village called Vadencourt on the Oise, north-west of Guise.

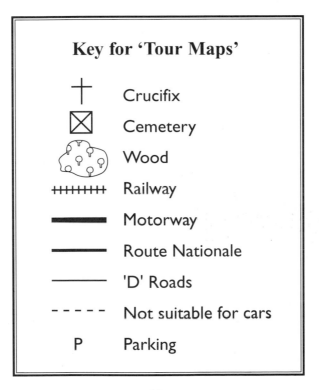

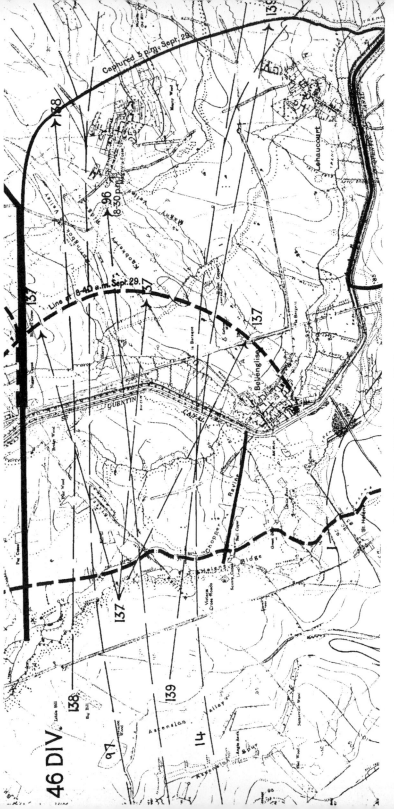

Attack of the 46th Division: 29 September 1918.

Chapter One

RIQUEVAL

Every operation in the slow, resolute advance of British and Dominion forces across the devasted lands of the Somme brought them nearer to the Hindenburg Line. This elaborate and extensive system of defence, supported by additional wire fields and deep trenches to its rear, was designed to be the breakwater against which the Allied advance would founder. German intent was that prolonged and costly battles against the lines would sap Allied will to continue the flight; war weariness and national bankruptcy would induce them to sue for peace. The arrival of American forces and the deteriorating situation on the German home front had, however, increased Allied resolution to continue until Germany was thoroughly defeated. The Hindenburg Line had been broken before, and thus could be again.

The battles of September 1918 brought the Allied line to within sight of, and in places into, the Hindenburg outpost lines. Time was needed to gather sufficient men and material to make the next, perhaps most significant assault. There was a slight pause on the sector opposite Bellenglise. A fresh division was brought up to replace the overworked and under-strength Australian divisions in the area between Bellenglise and Riqueval. They were to be given a short break

An aerial photo of Bellenglise taken in March 1917. Trenches snake their way towards the rear, the one in the centre passing to the left of the site of the village mill. Fields of barbed wire lie west of the canal. Many of the buildings are as yet intact and few shell holes scar the fields.

in order to allow for a token refitting, and were then to be deployed to assist two inexperienced American divisions a few thousand metres to the north. The 46th Division moved in to occupy the former Dominion positions such as Ascension Wood, Big and Little Bill and Victoria Crossroads. The 46th knew that it was to be the spearhead of the next attack, and it also knew the objective. What most of its men did not yet know was the extent of the difficulties they would encounter. This realisation came when they moved into their new positions and gazed upon the unappealing waters of the St. Quentin Canal.

In the months preceding September, the 46th (North Midland) Division had been used sparingly. It had avoided the fate of so many other divisions during the 1918 Battles of the Somme and the Lys. As part of Fifth Army, in August and early September it took part in the Flanders offensive and, mid way through the month, shifted down to the Somme. While at Sailly near Amiens the division rehearsed tactics for crossing canals and other stretches of water. The training was not taken particularly seriously, with the result that General Campbell was reported as being 'extremely disappointed'.[1] Further practice sessions for groups of men from 137 Brigade took place near Bihécourt on 27 September. These were stopped when too many enemy shells began

An Australian soldier views the German stronghold of Bellenglise from his trench near Bell Copse on 20 September 1918. IWM Q3390

landing among them. The parties removed to Brie on 28 September and met with rather more success.

Experienced troops of the division had come across European canals during their travels in France and Belgium. Very different from the narrow canals which linked the industrial Midlands, French ones were wider and deeper. Where it ran through a cutting north of Bellenglise, the St Quentin had an almost perpendicular embankment of 50 feet. The sides of the canal were in parts brick-lined and the water varied between 7 and 15 feet in depth. Its water was stagnant, fetid and, in sections where it was held back by concrete dams, the mud was deep and ineluctable. The waterway was 35 feet wide, with the banks almost bare of vegetation, and was an integral part of the Hindenburg Line defences. The outpost and canal banks bristled with machine-gun posts, the eastern defences had numerous concrete emplacements scattered among the deep trenches, while in Bellenglise there was a large shell-proof tunnel capable of sheltering 3,000 men; its exits could disgorge men directly into the trench system. German gunners to the rear had all possible approaches to the canal accurately registered. Captured German documents underlined the importance the enemy put on maintaining the position. Soldiers of the *38th Division* were promised extra rations an pay for every British prisoner they captured near the defences, while the line itself was

'considered to afford most favourable conditions for a

stubborn defence...it is an impregnable rampart...[and] must be held absolutely intact'.[2]

These German sentiments were echoed by many British observers. A diarist of the 8/Sherwood Foresters thought it a 'most unpromising position to attack – indeed, we thought it impregnable'.[3] Neither did Major-General Boyd make any attempt to conceal the dangers of the operation. He instructed Brigadier-General Campbell to inform his soldiers of the 'honourable but difficult'[4] task which lay ahead.

The key to a successful assault lay in the preparation. As the artillery's expertise grew, experience showed that a bombardment of the right intensity, duration and calibre of guns was often the deciding factor between success and failure. A careful and deliberate bombardment programme was developed as more and more guns were ushered into the crowded valleys to the west of Ste Hélène Ridge. According to one observer it was probably the 'largest array of guns that ever was collected'.[5] An intensive barrage lasting 48 hours would be fired by divisional and corps guns before the infantry went over. Harassing fire began on German positions on 26 September, and on the following day was supplemented by the increasingly intensive programme. Two 6-inch batteries were ordered to rest by day and fire one round per minute at night on the canal banks and Bellenglise. 18-pdr guns of 230 Brigade RFA fired 100 rounds per gun on two successive days; 4.5-inch howitzers of 231 Brigade expended 150 rounds per day. A regular supply of mustard gas was also liberally dropped on German trenches and known canal crossing-points during this preliminary period. Captured enemy maps helped the planners to pin-point the main positions and known assembly areas. It was decided that the infantry should attack behind a creeping barrage advancing at a rate of 100 yards every two minutes. When the barrage reached the Hindenburg Line (the Blue Line), it would pause for a few minutes and then lift to a 'safety' line for 30 minutes to allow the Blue Line to be consolidated. In addition to the field and heavy artillery, divisional trench-mortar batteries would fire a mixture of smoke and HE. The 36 guns of 46th Battalion MGC were supported by those of the 100th Battalion and the 2nd Life Guards Machine-Gun Battalion. The

The canal just north of Bellenglise. Troops of the 6/South Staffs used the plank bridges to effect their crossing.

This German light railway on the east side of the canal climbed the embankment and continued up Springbok Valley.

companies dug themselves into pits distributed along the eastern slopes of Ascension Valley, roughly from Watling Street north to Little Bill. The role of the machine-gunners was to fire a covering barrage above the heads of the attacking infantry. Section commanders were instructed to use 'boldness and determination' in their selection of targets and were allowed to divert from the main barrage if they saw suitable ones east of the canal. It was hoped two supply tanks would be available to carry forward ammunition but, if these failed, the 500 boxes of Vickers and 200 boxes of German bullets, along with 30 spare barrels and the equipment required for an advanced armourer's shop, would be carried by pack animals.

The huge numbers of men and guns moving into the assembly areas made heavy demands on local roads and equally heavy demands on the RE and Pioneers. Divisional Field Companies were required to dig shelters and gun pits, construct artillery and infantry trench bridges, peg tracks for pack animals and infantry, reconnoitre crossing points and select sites for future supply dumps, signal stations and HQ positions. They were assisted in their work by the divisional Pioneers, the 1/Monmouth. These often skilled men and labourers worked on roads, dug and carried forward the trench-mortar shells, barbed wire, telephone cables, cork bridges, collapsible boats and the thousand and one other things required for the assault. Huge piles of equipment ready for transporting forward to the canal were dumped round Battalion HQ near Victoria Crossroads. Collection and distribution of supplies was made easier when Canadian Railway Troops completed the relaying of the track between Roisel and Vermand. Lorries and GS wagons piled up and down through Villecholles, Bihécourt and

19

Vadencourt, where files of men waited to unload them and carry their cargoes forward. Further down the railway to the rear, three casualty clearing stations, the 12th, 50th (Northumbrian) and 53rd (North Midland) moved into Tincourt and began preparations to receive the anticipated wounded.

Numerous conferences of divisional and brigade staffs finally decided the infantry's scheme of attack. The assault was one of several designed to maintain momentum all along a front stretching from the Meuse to the coast. The Staffordshire Brigade would lead the attack on a front of less than 2000m. The canal would be crossed from a little north of the Vermand-Bellinglise road to Riqueval bridge. There would be no supporting attacks on either of the immediate flanks, although 1st Division on the right would make a 'demonstration' on the southern side of the canal. On the left there would be a gap of about 1200m between Riqueval bridge and the American and Australian sector to the north. 137 Brigade was to assault with the 5/North

British troops soon utilized the former German dugouts and shelters on the canal's western embankment. This photo shows Australian troops socialising, cooking and hanging washing out to dry a little south of the canal tunnel. IWM Q9525

Stafford on the left, 5/South Stafford in the centre and 6/South Stafford on the right. Each would have two companies up, with two passing through. Once the brigade had secured the Brown Line, 138 and 139 Brigades would leap-frog through onto the next objective. The North and South Staffords each detailed two platoons as mopping-up parties (these groups being supported by a company of the 8/SF attached to them for this purpose), and another two platoons as carrying parties. They would lug the heavier materials forward to the canal, assisted by a section of RE. The canal was to be crossed by the use of ropes, floating piers of petrol cans and cork slabs, collapsible boats and mud mats. In addition to his life jacket (3000 of which had been requisitioned from the cross-Channel leave boats), each man was to carry 120 rounds, two bombs and the usual rations.

An elaborate signalling scheme was devised in an attempt to lessen the inherent problems of communications during the advance. Tables detailing coloured flares for signals ranging from 'advanced cavalry troops here' to 'tank broken down' were distributed to battalions, men issued with reflective discs and told to indicate enemy positions to friendly aircraft by placing three rifles in a row. Contact aircraft would be recognised by a black rectangular board hanging from their fuselages. In order to maintain some sort of contact with the Americans to the north, 'exceptionally capable NCOs' were placed on the left of the 5/North Stafford, while the MGC was warned not to fire on anyone north of Riqueval bridge unless they were recognised as 'definitely German'.[6]

Before the assault on the canal could begin, the jumping-off positions needed to be improved. On 27 September 138 Brigade launched a successful attack from just east of Victoria Crossroads against the high ground north-east of Chopper Ravine. The brigade line now ran from Pike Wood, immediately north of Watling Street, to Bell Copse. There were still about 1500m to be crossed before the canal was reached, but it was all downhill. By 4.00am on 28 September, 137 Brigade had moved into the front positions in preparation for its attack. Unfortunately, the Germans were not content to allow the British to dictate events and launched a serious counter-attack against their former outposts. This preventative strike forced D Company of the 5/South Stafford into the trenches of the 5/North Stafford. C Company, sent up to reinforce the defenders, was hit by machine-gun fire as it moved down the slope south of Watling Street. Despite the arrival of fresh supplies of bombs, the Stafford could not eject the Germans from the captured posts. At 1.00pm Brigade decided to abandon the struggle and ordered the Stafford to remain where they were. Besides losing a few yards of trenches, the most disconcerting aspect of the operation was that the German penetration of the British positions revealing to them the boats, ladders and life jackets assembled for the following morning's attack.

Accounts vary as to the conditions at dawn on Sunday 29 September. The diarist of the 8/SF remembered it as 'a very dark night with mist'.[7] A member of 5/SF agreed, recalling that daylight 'dawned with heavy mist',[8] In contrast, an officer of the 6/South Stafford thought the 'clear brightness of dawn' 9 was revealed 'free even of the slightest mist'. A colleague in his sister battalion, the 5/South Stafford, also remembered there being no fog and a good clear light. What is certain, however, is that by the time the infantry went across, they did so in a thick fog.

Final preparations had gone on all through the night. In the rear, pack animals were harnessed, aid posts awaited their first wounded and everywhere was bustle and movement. Last minute stores were hauled through congested trenches, guides from each company of the support brigades attached themselves to the rear assaulting companies, men checked and rechecked their equipment, smoked endlessly, made nervous jokes or sought solace in their own thoughts. Above their heads the bombardment roared and thundered towards the German positions. Some men thought the rising mist to be a bad omen, others that it was some ingenious new form of smoke barrage. As the brigade lined up on its tapes at 5.20am, there was almost a pause in the shelling. The gunners were merely girding themselves for the final terrible onslaught. At 5.30am the barrage crashed out in an unimaginable crescendo of concentrated violence. Noise and pressure waves combined to stupefy the ears and brains of the waiting troops. Thousands of machine-gun bullets swished through the air; HE tore it asunder. Amid the pandemonium, the infantry groped their way through the all-pervading mist.

With visibility down to about four yards, direction was kept by compass. Men split up into small groups, infiltrating either deliberately or accidentally the outlying German posts, and reached the canal. Machine-gun fire had been erratic and, where posts were located, they were easily subdued. On the front of the 6/South Stafford, where the embankment was at its lowest and the canal largely bereft of water, many of the German footbridges were still astride the canal. The Staffordshiremen rushed across, regrouped and advanced on the Hindenburg Line itself. A 77mm field gun fired at them from point-blank range until its crew was overcome. The main line was crossed quite easily and the Staffords consolidated on the Brown Line some 200m to its east. There were still several bridges crossing the canal on the sector of the 5/South Stafford. The attackers reorganised on the west side and then crossed. On the northern flank, men scrambled down the embankment and paused while their officers swam across to secure ropes to the opposite bank. Others plunged into the murky water, relying on their life belts to see them safely across. Using whatever handholds from scrub an debris they could find, they hauled themselves up the banking to the trenches at the top. The mist still largely hid their progress from German eyes, although by this time the enemy was certainly fully awake to what was going on. On the extreme left, Captain Charlton of the 5th and a party of engineers from 466th Field Company stormed Pont Riqueval. Details of what happened next are confused. Most accounts credit Charlton with killing two Germans in the act of trying to blow the bridge. Another says that an NCO with Charlton shot four Germans as the officer cut the leads. A third claims that it was Corporal Openshaw RE who rushed at three Pioneers, bayonetted two of them and persuaded the third to reveal where the explosive charges were concealed. The corporal is then supposed to have accounted for a machine-gun post. Whatever the precise detail, the bridge was saved and secured.[10]

All storming parties were across the canal one hour after Zero. A German barrage had come down on the west bank but was never enough to stop the 'enthusiastic moral of our men'. 11 Troops from all three battalions had lost direction and crossed unit boundaries. Platoon and section commanders tried to restore some cohesion and organisation, but the mist still hampered their efforts. Groups pressed on up the slope through the Blue Line and on to the Brown. The mists also exacerbated the problems of communication: Lucas lamps were useless, runners lost their way, aircraft and flares were invisible. Battalion and brigade HQs depended largely on the often dubious evidence of wounded men passing on their way to the rear. However, on this occasion the wounded seemed to be in such high spirits and their stories so emphatic, that their testimony was believed. Confirmation of early success came when streams of German prisoners came back guarded by only nominal escorts; they all assured the questioning Stafford that the enemy line was broken. HQs moved to their prearranged forward positions and word was sent back to the support brigades to advance.

Having experienced great difficulty in finding their assembly positions in the lines vacated by the Staffordshires, 138 and 139 Brigades waited on Ste Hélêne Ridge for three hours. Direction from Ascension Ridge and Le Verguier was kept by compass, but companies became separated while negotiating the maze of old trenches, gun pits and transport lines filling Ascension Valley. The hope was that battalions would regroup in the old British line and then head off towards the canal. To complicate matters further, the CO and Adjutant of the 4/Leicester were both badly wounded and evacuated while leading their battalion towards the valley. The Adjutant of the nearby 5/Leicester lost in the fog not only one of his companies, but also his own horse. Eventually all companies of the 4th Battalion, with the exception of one platoon, were reported to be in position. The battalion's padre finally turned up leading the missing platoon through the murk. At 8.30 Brigade dispatched orders to advance, but because runners became lost, battalions did not receive them until an hour later. Still not convinced that they were in touch with units on their flanks, 138 Brigade headed for the left front and the Foresters' Brigade, the right.

Passing piles of wrecked equipment and numerous German corpses, the support battalions crossed the canal by wooden bridges, passed through the Staffords and moved on to the Yellow Line. There was stiff resistance from south of the canal and the many pill boxes in Bellenglise village. Lieutenant-Colonel Bernard Vann, the CO of the 6/SF, won the VC for rallying his men and leading them forward up the slope beyond Bellenglise. Enemy field guns fired at the Foresters over open sights and several conter-attacks, one led by a mounted officer, attempted to throw them back across the canal. Progress through Bellinglise was hindered by piles of rubble filling the streets. Sections and platoons gradually worked along the trenches lining the canal bank with bomb and bayonet. Smoke grenades blinded anti-tank gunners and strong points, the garrisons of which showed an increasing propensity to surrender in large numbers. Groups of bewildered, incoherent and dazed Germans willingly gave themselves up to individual soldiers. They were allotted wounded to carry or help and sent back across the canal. In the opposite direction tanks waddled and clattered towards Bellenglise, horse transport waited for the roads to clear and guns were limbered up ready for movement across the canal. Parties of RE and Pioneers were already hard at work clearing obstructions, making rough repairs to existing bridges and transforming several of the concrete dams into causeways for GS wagons. Engineers were also exploring the length of the enormous

Bellenglise tunnel. Many Germans had not emerged from its confines until the Staffords were upon them. From a place of safety it was transformed into a veritable trap. Engineers soon located the tunnel;s electric-light plant and with the help of German operatives had restarted it by 30 September. The whole operation had gone so well that at 9.30am on the first day Major-General Boyd asked for troopers of 5 Cavalry Brigade to be sent forward. However, as was so often the case, the cavalry had such difficulty in forcing a passage through the congested roads that by the time it reached the forward zone, its opportunity had gone.

The Sherwood Foresters and the Leicesters to their north pushed on towards the Black Line. The amount of debris strewn amidst the ruins of Bellenglise, as well as German resistance, continued to delay the advance. Nevertheless, the 8/Sherwood Foresters reached its objective only a little behind schedule and its 6th Battalion leap-frogged through. Fire from south of the canal caught the Foresters in enfilade but the 1st Division seemed to have exerted enough pressure on the Germans to force them to limit the strength and number of their objective. The 6th Battalion established posts in Lehaucourt by 1.30pm and was leap-frogged by its 5th Battalion in the early afternoon. The final objective, the Black Line, was about 500m east of Lehaucourt. German resistance stiffened as the 5th fought its way on across the fields and enemy gun pits. One company followed the canal bank and faced intense opposition from machine guns and a 77mm gun near the Lehaucourt bridge. A patrol was even sent across the canal to eliminate the crew of a field gun which was firing on their flank through open sights. The village of Lehaucourt was not too badly knocked about and, once the protecting machine-gun crews had been silenced, often by the bayonet, the Foresters pressed on 'chasing the enemy out of the trenches like rabbits out of a hedgerow'.[12] The village itself was secured and by 5.00pm the 5th Battalion had halted on its objective a little to the east.

A patrol of the 5/Leicester had entered Lehaucourt from its western

British troops amid the wreckage of Bellenglise, 4 October 1918.

end at about 2.30pm. Following the confusion experienced as they had formed up west of the canal some hours before, the Leicesters had crossed in the wake of 137 Brigade and advanced up the slope towards Magny-la-Fosse. The 4th Battalion had reached its objective and the 5/Lincoln passed through. Despite being shelled from point blank range, the 5/Leicester secured its objective opposite Merville Old Mill on top of the Lehaucourt Ridge. A German field gun was seen to be limbering up a few score metres in front and part of C Company took off in pursuit. Running through their own barrage, the Leicesters captured the gun as its crew fled. For several minutes another German battery in Levergies fired upon the batttalion's right flank, causing 'considerable inconvenience'.[13] C Company, consolidating in a sunken road running through the site of the mill, suffered most from its close-range fire. D Company advanced as far as Fosse Wood and began to dig in on a line stretching from the wood's western face, north to the crest of the Magny – Joncourt road. The extreme left was in vague touch with the Australians, while the right had contacted with the 5/Sherwood Foresters in Lehaucourt.

During the late afternoon the van battalions of the 46th Division waited for the 32nd Division to come through and continue the advance. Meanwhile, they consolidated their gains and sorted out their mixed platoons. The HQ of the 5/Leicester was bombed by a British plane and the Reverend Buck, who had done such good work in reuniting the dispersed battalion in the fog of the early morning, was killed whilst he and the Medical Officer tried to bring in some wounded tank crews. The tanks had played a useful role in assisting the infantry, but the battlefield between Bellenglise and Magny was strewn

The incongruous scene of 137 Brigade's band playing amid the devastation of Bellenglise.

with at least ten of their abandoned hulls.

At about 5.30pm units of the 32nd Division began to appear in the area taken by 138 and 139 Brigades. Unfortunately, the build-up of traffic in Bellenglise had delayed their advance and by the time the leading battalions had taken over the Foresters' and Leicesters' positions, it was generally considered too late in the day to attempt any further operations. Strong enemy fire came from Joncourt to the north and Levergies to the south, but a chronicler of the 8/Sherwood Foresters later noted that: 'There is no doubt that could their attack have been pushed on at once the fighting of the next few days would have been unnecessary'.[14] This comment was perhaps a little optimistic, especially as the 8th was by the late afternoon considerably to the rear of the front positions. Furthermore, even if the 32nd had succeeding in creating some openings in the Fonsomme Line, the cavalry were still held up in and around Bellenglise and would have been unable to exploit any gaps made.

An additional factor which militated against a possible breakthrough was the Corps Commander's knowledge that the 32nd Division's artillery would not be in place to fire a barrage until at least 6.00pm. Cooperation between the New Army and the Territorial divisions had been close, even to having adjacent HQ in Small Foot Wood. The purpose of such proximity was that, in the words of the official historian, the 32nd Division would be in a position to 'seize the right moment to go through'.[15] A divisional report had suggested with some enthusiasm that:

> 'Through it was clear that [Sequehart], being in a strong commanding position, was likely to be stoutly held by the enemy, it was hoped that it might be captured by a rapid advance, following on the surprise of the strong defences of the canal'[16]

Unfortunately, although the 32nd passed over the canal from its assembly positions around Vendelles and Le Verguier as rapidly as the general confusion allowed, it was to be too late for anything significant to be achieved and Sequehart would remain in German hands for another week.

On the left of the 32nd Division's front, 97 Brigade, led by the 5/Border and 2/KOYLI, headed slightly left after crossing the canal at Bellenglise. The Borderers advanced towards Magny-la-Fosse but the tanks they had been promised failed to materialise. The left of the battalion was exposed to heavy fire from south of Joncourt and from the southern slopes of Mill Ridge largely because the Australians and Americans had experienced such difficulties in taking the canal tunnel to the north of IX Corps. The Borderers were stopped a little to the north-east of Magny and began to dig in for the night.

On the right, and despite equally heavy fire, the 2/KOYLI had moved quickly to cross the spurs which commanded the village of Levergies. Captain Pring seized the high ground to its right and a battery of four guns, while Captain Cass spotted another battery in the process of withdrawing its guns. Cass's fire was immediately returned by a third battery only some 2000m away. He responded by leading two platoons in a charge which resulted in the capture of the enemy guns. Germans were seen to be pulling back into the village, but with the light fading and the general situation rather obscure, the KOYLI also dug in.

The third battalion of 97 Brigade, the 10/Argyll and Sutherland Highlanders, crossed at Riqueval at 3.45pm and were close to Magny by 5.30pm. Although Brigade was concerned about the Australians' lack of progress, the GSO2, whom the Argylls' CO met soon after crossing the canal, insisted that the battalion get on as far as it could towards the Beaurevoir Line. This opinion was confirmed by the brigadier when he came up to observe the situation. Consequently, their companies pushed on with great determination and immediately came under heavy fire from the left. They finally sought refuge in a sunken road south-east of Joncourt, in contact with the 5/Border on their right and with the Australians on their rear left flank. The night of continuous heavy rain and considerable shelling was spent in the most decided salient ever occupied by the CO during nearly three years' of service in France'.[17]

The 1/Dorsets and 15/HLI of 14 Brigade had crossed at Bellenglise, coming under fairly heavy fire from machine guns on the higher ground to the south. Once across they fanned right. Le Tronquoy was taken and two companies of the Dorsets captured Fleche Wood. The wood produced nearly 400 prisoners, three 12-inch howitzers, five 4.2-inch field guns and five machine guns. Another company, to the right of the KOYLI, attained the high ground south of Levergies but as it was 8.30pm, and unsure of its flanks, the company withdrew to the lower slopes. That evening darkness drew a cold, misty cloak around defender and attacker alike; its job for the time being done, the 46th Division prepared to leave the field to its more recent arrivals.

On relief the battalions of the 46th Division could take stock of their day's success. The haul of prisoners, machine guns and trench mortars had been astounding, and their own losses relatively light. They had smashed through the Hindenburg line and were now swarming all over former German trenches and concrete emplacements. Transport and guns moved forward; the Divisional General was observed with pennon flying and immaculately groomed horse; salvage teams scavenged at debris; signallers ran miles of cable between HQ; supply tanks lumbered forward to empty their hulls of wire, screw pickets and SAA; and above it all, flimsy aircraft buzzed around directing artillery shoots and strafing retreating troops. To the rear, a diarist of the 1/1 North Midland Field Ambulance noted with obvious satisfaction:

> 'Our casualties were small...German prisoners coming through in shoals...There were more Germans than British soldiers about the dressing station'.[18]

Firmer contact was eventually made with the Americans and Australians on the left who had experienced considerably more difficulty in breaching their sections of the Hindenburg Line. Many Americans had in fact become so lost and leaderless that they attached themselves to brigades of the 46th Division.

Flushed with their success and now some way to the rear, the North Midlanders began to settle down for the night. The HQ of the 5/Sherwood Foresters was established in a plushy furnished bunker, formerly the home of a German artillery brigade HQ. The previous owners had added to their comfort by providing a lavishly stocked larder and cellar. Officers of the 5th could reflect upon their success and good luck in some luxury. A little to the north, their fellow officers of the 5/Leicester had also ensconced themselves in a former artillery HQ. Unfortunately all they had to celebrate their success was to be greeted by a bunker 'very full of flies and other insects'.[19]

Three cheery Australians of the 9th Battalion enjoy a dubious 'wash' in the murky waters of the canal three days after its seizure. IWM E3492

Notes

1. *The War History of the 6th South Staffordshire Regiment*, (no author) p.215
2. *The Story of the Fourth Army in the Battles of the Hundred Days*
3. W. Weetman, *The 1/8th Sherwood Foresters in the Great War*, p.262
4. War Diary of 5/South Stafford. WO. 95.2686
5. Weetman, op.cit. p.262
6. War Diary of 46th Bn MGC. WO. 95.2686
7. Weetman, op.cit. p.263
8. L.de Grave, *The War History of the 5th Sherwood Foresters*, p.177
9. *The War History of the 6th South Staffordshire Regiment*, p.216
10. Corporal Openshaw's role in the affair is described in a letter written by Lt-Col Garforth, a/CRE 46th Division, appended to War Diary of 465th Field Company. WO. 95.2676
11. War Diary of 5/South Stafford. WO. 95.2686
12. L. de Grave, op.cit. p. 180
13. War Diary of 5/Leicester. WO.95.2690
14. Weetman, op.cit. p271
15. *O.H.* 1918 Vol. V. p. 105
16. Cited in *The History of the Dorset Regiment*, p.135
17. War Diary of 10/Argyll & Sutherland Highlanders. WO.95.2402
18. War Diary of 1/1st North Midland Field Ambulance. WO.95.2680
19. War Diary of 5/Leicester, op.cit.

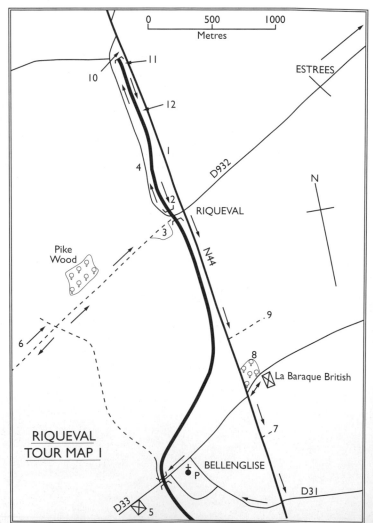

RIQUEVAL
TOUR MAP I

Riqueval Today
(Tour Map 1)

The canal cutting approaching the southern entrance to the tunnel remains an impressive piece of engineering. Its sides retain their often sheer drop and are today covered with considerably more vegetation than in 1918. Once the leaves have fallen, an arboreal promenade along either bank between the bridge and the tunnel allows good views of the canal. There remain several concrete structures, for example a machine-gun post where the slope from the *Rampe Impériale* car park joins the towpath and a recently excavated post on the west side above the tunnel portal. There are also machine-gun posts on the western embankment but these are usually covered by undergrowth. A canal museum stands above the tunnel entrance. This building survived, albeit only just, the ravages of war. A memorial to the troops from Tennessee who fought near the spot is just south of the car park. **(11)**

Riqueval is really only three

Riqueval bridge today, repaired but little changed from the way it looked in September 1918.

British troops marching across Riqueval bridge, 2 October 1918.
IWM Q9511

The southern portal of the tunnel, south of Bellicourt. A machine-gun aperture can be seen on the left but the steps up to the chamber have been bricked in.

Ernst Jünger

cottages and a *Routiers* café. A lone house sits in front of a quarry 400m north of the café on the east side of the N44. **(1)** In 1918 this housed an elaborate system of dugouts, some of which were used as dressing stations. It was used by the British in October as a cemetery for 35 Australian and British troops. Two very solid blockhouses guard the eastern end of Pont Riqueval and a memorial to the success of the Staffordshire Brigade has recently been erected nearby. Bridge Wood grows once again alongside the eastern end of Watling Street. This sunken lane joins a minor road immediately west of the bridge. This road leads up past Riqueval Farm and joins the N44 just north of the museum. The farm was used as a billet by Ernst Jünger in 1917. **(4)**

The village of Bellenglise, which was adopted by Stafford after the war, is much like most other villages in the area. It comprises a particularly unimaginative church, a *Mairie*, a café named *Chez Eric*, several farms and some housing near the canal. The communal cemetery is west of the canal on the Vermand road and contains the graves of 30 French soldiers killed in August 1914. **(5)**

A modern memorial commemorating the success of the 46th Division has been erected close to a German pill box guarding the eastern end of the bridge.

The canal is bordered by grain elevators on its western bank and from behind the silos a lane leads up to Watling Street and the 4th Australian Division's memorial. **(6)** The 46th Division's memorial is on the site of Bellenglise mill, 50m to the east of the N44. **(7)** La Baraque British Cemetery is 100m east of the N44 on a minor road to Joncourt. In the copse opposite the cemetery entrance are two German bunkers and a very dangerous vertical shaft. **(8)** These were used by the 46th Division on 29 September and the area around them was soon developed into RE dumps, aid stations and signalling posts. A quarry a few hundred yards north-east is reached by a track from the main road. It too was a German command centre but is now used extensively by fly-tippers. **(9)**

The grain silos at Bellenglise wharf. The southern flank of 137 Brigade's attack was at about this point. Here the canal has no significant embankment but the width of the trench and its lining of mud and water made it difficult going for the attackers of the 6/South Staffs.

Tour of Riqueval
(Tour Map 1)
9.7kms, 6miles. 2.25hours

Leave the car in the parking area beside Bellenglise church and the *salle des fêtes*. Take the D33 down to the canal and cross by the bridge. Turn right and follow the track up behind the grain silos to the 4th Australian Division memorial. Retrace your steps for 300m until you come to the T-junction where you turned left to the memorial. Go straight over. Watling Street is still sunken

Sitting high upon the Buisson Ridge, the memorial to the 4th Australian Division looks down on the land captured by the division and the jumping-off positions of the 46th Division. The plaque records the actions in which it participated during its three years in France and Belgium.

Looking north-east from close to the Australian memorial, this shot shows Pike Wood on the left and Watling Street, right and centre, running down to Bridge Wood.

The memorial to fallen soldiers of the state of Tennessee. The 30th (US) Division, or 'The old Hickory Division' as it was familiarly known, was formed of National Guard units from Tennessee and the Carolinas.

and very overgrown. Keep to the south of it by walking in the field. This patch is very rarely used to grow arable crops. After 300m drop down onto the lane itself. As you follow the gentle slope down towards the canal, Pike Wood is on your left. When the lane appears to fade out, keep to its northern side; the alternative is to end up in a wood and stumble down a steep bank. Keep going and Bridge Wood (3) joins the track on the right after another 300m.

At the bridge, walk along the west side of the embankment until you reach the tunnel mouth. The recently-excavated blockhouse is at the end of the path (10) and the museum just beyond the fence. The memorial to the soldiers from Tennessee is immediately south of the car park. (11)

Drop down to the eastern towpath. A machine-gun post guards the towpath at its junction with the *Rampe Impériale*. (12) Climb up to the promenade and follow it along to the bridge. The remains and lines of German trenches can be discerned just above the path. Two concrete bunkers and the recent memorial are on the

This German machine-gun post was built into the batter of the canal embankment just where the path from the *Rampe Impériale* descends onto the towpath. Its defenders could fire along the bank in the direction of Riqueval bridge.

bridge's eastern side. You are advised against dropping down to the towpath to Bellenglise. The eastern side is passable in winter but from spring to autumn it is a jungle of nettles and brambles. The western towpath disappears about 700m south of the bridge. It is easier to leave the canal at the bridge and walk down the N44 towards Bellenglise. In the copse immediately north of the small road to Joncourt (1 mile from the bridge) are two German concrete blockhouses. **(8)** Do not enter the copse from its western face but turn left up the Joncourt road and enter it from the field and its eastern edge. There is an uncovered vertical shaft near to its western edge. In summer it is covered by undergrowth and very difficult to spot. If you fall down that and live, you will be examining the German shelters which formed part of the underground labyrinth of defences.

Visit La Baraque British Cemetery and then walk down the N44 to the 46th Division memorial.(350m) There is a large bunker sunken to field level 40m south of the memorial, and another, smaller one, closer to the road. Continue south on the N44 until the turning right to Bellenglise. The road follows residential housing until it joins the car park. Alternatively, follow the N44 down to the canal. A German machine-gun post was tunnelled into the bridge abutment. Its entrance is in the trees on the eastern side of the road. Follow the towpath round until the bridge where the D33 crosses the canal.

The memorial to the 46th Division, erected on the former site of Bellenglise Mill. The obelisk was rather neglected over the years but is now in a better state of repair.

The unmistakable shape of German bunkers lurking in the copse immediately north of La Baraque British Cemetery. These were captured and put to use by units of the 46th Division.

Chapter Two

THROUGH BELLENGLISE AND BEYOND

Infantry units of the 46th Division spent 30 September resting. They remained largely in the areas captured the previous day, suffering some discomfort from intermittent German shelling. The 46th MG Battalion lost two killed and four wounded during the day, but overall, casualties were light. Having worked almost continuously for 48 hours the Pioneers of the 1/Monmouth were called upon to labour for only four hours. Their comrades in the Field Companies were more heavily engaged in bridge building and in exploring the underground tunnels in and around Bellenglise. The divisional signals section was busy laying cables and the gunners of 230 Brigade were fully occupied in moving forward the gun and wagon lines. They were expecting to be called upon to give supporting fire to the attacks of the 32nd Division but, despite being in their new positions and ready for action by noon,

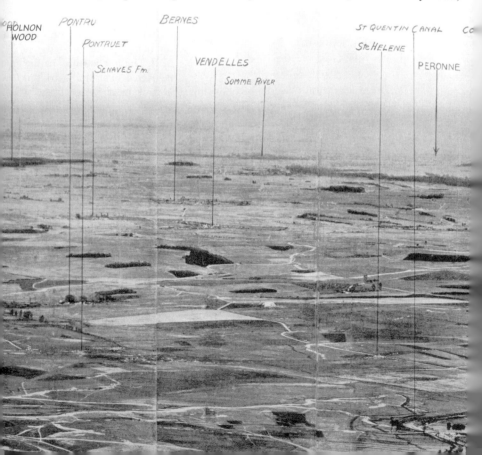

their services were not required. Nevertheless, the unit lost two killed
and 32 wounded during the course of the day. The Field Ambulances
continued to deal with wounded from the previous day and with those
of the 32nd Division who were in the process of evacuation down the
Vermand road.

The success or otherwise of the 32nd Division's assaults on 30
September depended to a great degree on whether the Australians on
the left and 1st Division on the right could get up on the flanks. The
task of 3 Brigade was to go for the hamlet of Thorigny and the trouble
spot of Talana Hill **(6)**; 1 Brigade was to attack on the low ground
between the hill and the canal. A similar attempt the previous day had
resulted in heavy casualties from enfilade fire from the hill. To help
them, the right of the 32nd Division was ordered to secure those
sections of Le Tronquoy canal tunnel not taken by the 15/HLI on the
29th, and a significant number of additional heavy guns were to add
their weight to an already impressive array of calibres. The 1st
Division's right flank was supposed to be protected by the advance of
the French XV Corps above St Quentin.

At 8.00am on 30 September the 15/Lancashire Fusiliers began what

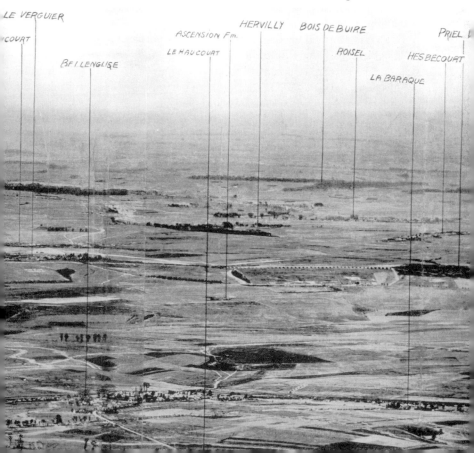

was destined to become a series of repeated attacks on Joncourt. To its left the Australian 32nd Battalion, unsupported by tanks or artillery, fought its way to within a few hundred metres of the village. The wire was obscured by long grass and self-sown crops and fire from the German positions in Cabaret Wood Farm **(1)** and the sugar factory **(2)** on the Estrées road further hampered the advance. The Fusiliers, who in a previous incarnation had begun life as the 1st Salford Pals, succeeded in establishing themselves in the outskirts of the village. The barrage had moved on too quickly but the Fusiliers were in touch with the Australians and with 97 Brigade on their right.

The day had begun disastrously for A Company of the 10/A&SH which occupied the head of the salient in Joncourt Trench to the south of the village. The company was attacked by hordes of Germans who advanced under a heavy machine-gun barrage. The company was surrounded and the HQ captured. The very few survivors scrambled back to trenches in the rear for safety and shelter.

Small parties of the 2/KOYLI pushed on towards Levergies during the morning of the 30th but orders for a major attack on the village arrived at HQ about 6.30pm. News that the attack was scheduled for 7.00pm aroused great consternation. However, under gathering darkness and the cover of a brief bombardment, Captain Cass of the 2/KOYLI rushed his company through the northern half of the village and out the other side for a loss of only eight dead and 55 wounded. For their work on this and the previous day Captains Cass and Pring were awarded the DSO. The southern part of the village was taken by the 1/Dorset of 14 Brigade, who then advanced as far as Pony Copse; this yielded 400 prisoners to the two battalions. Le Tronquoy tunnel was cleared and 3 Brigade secured Talana Hill with surprisingly little difficulty. The day's successes did little however to please the Commander-in-Chief. Haig complained to Foch that the task of taking the hill should properly have been the responsibility of General

Debeney's reluctant XV Corps rather than of his own tired 1st Division.

The misty dawn which heralded the daylight hours of 1 October soon evaporated and allowed the RAF to do some useful work during the subsequent operations. Fortunately the troublesome obstacles of Cabaret Wood Farm and the sugar factory had been overcome; this allowed the Australian 32nd Battalion to get its patrols into Joncourt from the north-west. An early reconnaissance by Major Mandleberg MC of the 15/LF revealed that the Germans had evacuated the village during the night, leaving only seven men to be captured by the Fusiliers and Australians. An attack on Preselles and the adjoining Chataignies Wood **(4)** by the 5/Border succeeded in getting into the hamlet, but frontal and enfilade fire forced it to withdraw to the railway cutting about 100m west of the wood. At about the same time the 5/6 Royal Scots and Dorsets had a go at the strategically important village of Sequehart. Although small in size it perched atop a significant rise, commanding all the ground to the east, south and west.

At 1.00am the Dorsets were informed that they would attack the village at 6.25am that morning. Keeping close to the barrage, the battalion was through the streets by 7.45am. Fifteen minutes later the Germans counter-attacked and, despite a bayonet charge by one company, the Dorsets were forced back to the western edge. At 4.00pm it was the turn of the 5/6 Royal Scots to attempt its capture, their attack being part of a coordinated assault involving the 5th Australian Division to the north. The Scots advanced from Levergies, swept through Sequehart and captured over 150 prisoners. But, as the battalion's chronicler later recalled, that evening the Germans 'revealed some of their old form'.[1] A counter-attack on both flanks forced the Scots back to a line some 200m west of the village.[2]

Supported by eight tanks, the main thrust of the afternoon attack was carried out by the 2/Manchester of 96 Brigade. The object of

the attack was to penetrate and then exploit any gaps made in the Beaurevoir–Fonsomme Line. While nowhere near as formidable or complete as the Hindenburg system to the east, its thick wire and two shallow lines of trenches were heavily reinforced by concrete machine-gun nests sited about every 50m to give mutual covering fire. The Manchesters attacked at 4.00pm

Australians receiving intstructions prior to an attack.

and, despite some very thick wire and heavy fighting, made good progress. By 7.00pm they were through the wire, over the trenches of the Beaurevoir Line and had taken the German strong point of Swiss Cottage **(5)** on the left. For a loss of a dozen dead and under 90 wounded the battalion had made a substantial penetration of the enemy defences and captured 200 prisoners. The real disappointment had been on 97 Brigade's front. The Argylls had moved forward into the trenches vacated by the 5/Border when that battalion had advanced on Chataignies Wood. The Argylls' CO was called to Brigade and told that next morning at 8.30am his battalion would be required to succeed where the Borders had failed.

The *Official History* notes tersely that on 2 October 'no progress worth mention' was made.[3] The ground captured that day was certainly minimal but, for troops of the 32nd Division, it was yet another bloody twenty-four hours. The onus fell on them because on the left flank the 50th (Northumbrian) and 2nd Australian Divisions were in the process of relieving the 3rd and 5th Australian Divisions respectively. On the right the 1st Division was required only to keep in touch with the slow-moving French, yet despite not being actively engaged, the 1/LNL and 1/Cameron Highlanders of 1 Brigade suffered many casualties from shell fire on Le Tronquoy–Sequehart Ridge. The pause in effort either side of the 32nd Division was perhaps not appreciated by the division itself but it did provide a welcome breathing space for the supply services. Such was the array of artillery that 15 ammunition trains per day were having to be cleared at Templeux-le-Guérard railhead. Shells then had to be transported by wagon or pack mules the five miles along congested roads to Bellenglise where the bulk of IX Corps artillery was sited.

Many of the shells brought up the previous day and night ended up on Ramicourt and Sequehart. The former village was assaulted by 96 Brigade who, forming up east of Joncourt, crossed the Beaurevoir Line despite receiving heavy fire from positions opposite the inactive Australian division on its left. No one seems to have informed the 18th Battalion on the right of the Australian Corps that the 32nd Division was to make an attack; as a consequence, the 2nd Australian Division did not cooperate. The Australian official historian decided that 'like so many other hurried local efforts to exploit a supposed chance of breaking through, the thrust failed'.[4] Nevertheless, 96 Brigade pressed on. With the death of Lieutenant-Colonel Stone, the CO of the 16/LF, and several of his officers, confusion reigned until Lieutenant Lewis delivered a report which convinced the brigadier that troops east of the

Beaurevoir–Fonsomme Line should withdraw and stand fast in the line itself. Ramicourt had not been taken but a foothold had been reasonably well established in the Beaurevoir Line. The two Fusilier battalions of 96 Brigade earned a DSO, a bar to a DSO, four MCs, one DCM and 16 MMs for their work that day.

The 5/6 Royal Scots had yet another go at Sequehart, with much the same result as on the previous day. The Scots swept into the village and called up three companies of the 15/HLI to protect their flanks. Three hours later the Germans fell upon the battalion's left and overwhelming numbers again forced it to retire. When he heard that the enemy was once more pouring through the streets, Second Lieutenant Davidson Smith, who was receiving attention to a knee wound, limped back to rally his men but fell shortly after. The Scots took 280 prisoners, 30 machine guns and three field guns, but the village remained in German hands.

The division's third Scottish battalion, the 10/A&SH, also had an active and disappointing day. One company attacked the trenches to the north of Chataignies Wood and succeeded in entering the Beaurevoir Line. Twenty Germans were killed in hand-to-hand fighting but the Argylls had themselves sustained ten fatalities. The party came under enfilade fire from further down the trench and was forced to seek shelter in a dugout from which it was unable to emerge with safety until nightfall. Another company went for the wood itself but as the barrage had concentrated on the wood rather than the trenches either side, flanking fire tore into the attackers. Progress became impossible and the remnant of the company withdrew and joined the 5/Border sheltering on the railway embankment.

When the fighting, save for artillery exchanges, died down for the night, IX Corps held a front of 8000m from Le Tronquoy to Swiss Cottage on the road mid way between Joncourt and Ramicourt. It thus occupied the high ground from Le Tronquoy to just west of Sequehart and to about 1000m north-west of Preselles. From there to Swiss Cottage, lodgements had been made in the Beaurevoir Line. On a more positive note, later intelligence reports suggested that the enemy had been compelled to rush up reserves from south of St Quentin to confront the threat posed by the corps.

After the relative quiet of 2 October, Corps decided upon a major effort for the following day. On 2 October members of 137 Brigade had returned to the scene of their earlier triumph and posed, complete with life jackets, for the camera and their brigadier on the canal bank. The Foresters' Brigade had spent two fairly quiet nights and days in former

German dugouts in Lehaucourt and Springbok Valley, while 138 Brigade had rested near Bellenglise. The artillery brigades had been out of action since 1 October and had spent their time resting and overhauling the weapons. Their guns and HQ were taken forward during the late afternoon of 2 October. During the following night 137 and 139 Brigades moved up to take over about half the front held by the 32nd Division. The North Midland Brigades slotted in between the 32nd and the 2nd Australian Division on the right. Having been in action since 29 September, the 32nd Division was exhausted. Its ranks were filled by young soldiers, many of whom had not previously seen action and who had undergone over three days of gruelling fighting sustained by little food and inadequate shelter. It was therefore with great relief that several battalions headed towards the dugouts and extensive catacombs of Levergies and Lehaucourt.

Orders for the attack of 137 and 139 Brigades were given to company commanders at a hastily arranged conference at about 10.00pm on 2 October. Their companies faced a march of between three and four miles to reach the jumping-off tapes. This in itself was no mean task as in the gloom of a murky October night they had first to find the tapes; they were usually found in sunken lanes in a countryside crisscrossed by sunken lanes. There was no time for any reconnaissance and none of the battalions had been in the sector before. In view of the difficulties, it was quite remarkable that all units were in the correct position before the barrage opened.

The Germans seemed to have anticipated the attack and during the forming-up period deluged the areas around Joncourt and Levergies

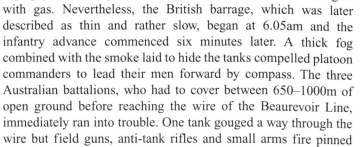

with gas. Nevertheless, the British barrage, which was later described as thin and rather slow, began at 6.05am and the infantry advance commenced six minutes later. A thick fog combined with the smoke laid to hide the tanks compelled platoon commanders to lead their men forward by compass. The three Australian battalions, who had to cover between 650–1000m of open ground before reaching the wire of the Beaurevoir Line, immediately ran into trouble. One tank gouged a way through the wire but field guns, anti-tank rifles and small arms fire pinned down most of the 18th and 17th Battalions in front of the line. Lieutenant Joseph Maxwell of the 18th Battalion led his company through the wire and then killed the crews of two machine guns. He was subsequently captured but escaped by shooting his guards and regained his own line. He was awarded the VC. However, the failure of the Australians to get forward allowed the German defenders in

Lieutenant Joseph Maxwell

42

Wiancourt to pour a deadly fire into the left flank of 139 Brigade. The 8/Sherwood Foresters detached two companies to successfully assault the village from the rear. Although still not quite in touch, the 17th Australian Battalion then passed through.

As the bombardment had failed to blow any significant gaps in the wire or to silence the numerous concrete machine-gun nests, the Foresters had enough difficulties of their own without having to detail men to take the Australians' objectives. The bayonet was used by many to quell the garrisons and on two such occasions Sergeant Johnson of the 5/SF single-handedly rushed the posts and dispatched their crews. He was awarded the VC for his gallantry. Even when the Foresters passed through the

Sergeant William Henry Johnson

Beaurevoir Line, their work was really only just beginning. Scores of machine guns were hidden in pits and concrete emplacements behind the forward line and they too were usually taken by the bayonet. Meanwhile, the supporting tanks were being knocked out by guns firing over open sights and all became casualties. One leviathan managed to destroy 16 machine-gun nests before it too became a victim of German fire. The Foresters forged on, entered Ramicourt (where to their surprise they were embraced by French civilians) and passed through towards Montbrehain. It was at Ramicourt that Colonel Vann leading the 6/SF was killed.(5)

While waiting for the barrage to move on, the Foresters sorted out their mixed battalions and companies. Then continued the advance. Montbrehain was reached and cleared by 11.30am, but casualties had been heavy and dismounted troopers of 5 Cavalry Brigade were brought up to the Beaurevoir Line in support. Furthermore, a gap of nearly a mile had developed between the right of 139 Brigade and the Staffords on the left.

The Stafford battalions had fought their way through the wire of the Beaurevoir Line and on towards Mannequin Hill. **(3)** Like the Foresters they too had made prodigious use of the bayonet, a factor which, although applauded by their commanders, at times created additional problems.[6] The crest of the hill was reached and outposts established but the gap between the two North Midland brigades and another one between the right of the Staffords and the 32nd Division invited retaliation.

Meanwhile the 32nd Division was having another go at Sequehart – or what was left of it. A British barrage fell on the village for ten consecutive hours before 14 Brigade advanced yet again. A combination of battalions, the 1/Dorsets, 15/HLI and 5/6 Royal Scots (supported by the 2/KOYLI of 97 Brigade working down from the north and the 1/LNL of 1 Brigade to the south) forced their way through the ruins and out to the fields beyond. It was however, too late to save the exposed Midlanders on Mannequin Hill and in Montbrehain. In the face of determined counter-attacks and with both flanks still in the air, the Foresters were compelled to withdraw from Montbrehain. The Staffords were also under extreme pressure on the hill and had to follow suit.[7] Both brigades established a line running north-west–south-east between Ramicourt and Montbrehain, with a defensive flank thrown back south-west to join with the 32nd Division east of Sequehart.

An historian of the 5/SF doubted whether the battalion had ever spent a more miserable night than that of 3-4 October. The one consoling factor was that 'exhaustion was so complete that even the wet, followed by frost, allowed, if not sleep, at all events stupor'.[8] German shells crashed all around their positions during the night and the following day. Men of the 2/KOYLI spent the day being sniped at by field guns as they lay in exposed positions east of Sequehart; further back the 10/A&SH, now only 250 strong, continued to lose men from a deluge of gas drenching the area west of the village. The long, showery day dragged by and the troops in the forward positions hoped for relief. During the darkness of 4-5 October, and after what seemed an eternity of torment, the 46th Division was relieved by the Australians and the 1st Division. The North Midlanders made their very weary way back to the familiar folds of Ascension Valley.

The intensity of the fighting had caused heavy casualties. Even the 46th MG Battalion had lost 21 killed and nearly 100 wounded, while the Pioneers of the 1/Monmouth, who had been brought up the line east of Ramicourt during 3 October, had 15 killed and over 60 wounded. In the divisional artillery, all but one of 230 Brigade's signal detachment were killed or wounded when its HQ was shelled and gassed on the 4th. It was, however, among the infantry that the casualties were most severe. Two battalion commanders, Colonel Vann of the 6/SF and Colonel Evans of the 6/North Staffords, had been killed and three others wounded. Evans' battalion returned to bivvies in Ascension Valley with a fighting strength of 11 officers and 356 men; it had arrived there seven days earlier with 24 officers and 794 other ranks. Yet, given the ferocity of the fighting and the depth of the defences it had been forced to penetrate, the number of dead compares favourably with its experience at the Hohenzollern and its disastrous attack at Gommecourt.[9]

Gommecourt had been a major defeat for the 46th Division but now, as a delighted officer of the 5/Leicester noted:

'After three and a half years the 46th Division has at last made a name for itself, and its doings on 29 September are known all the world over'.[10]

Indeed, congratulations for their efforts at Bellenglise and Riqueval had been pouring in to the HQ of the Stafford Brigade during the intervening period. Army, corps and divisional commanders all praised the achievement. Rawlinson called it a 'very fine performance', the GOC 1st Division 'a magnificent performance', and there were many others in similar vein. However, perhaps the most telling and appreciated was that received from the Walsall Branch of the National Federation of Discharged and Demobilised Sailors and Soldiers. The branch expressed

'...its great admiration of the wonderful deeds of the 46th Division who, on 29 September, crossed the Scheldt Canal, smashed the Hindenburg Line... [and] achieved the most glorious victory of any division in this war'.[11]

These were men who had served with the division at the Hohenzollern, Gommecourt and elsewhere. They had since carried with them the contemporary stigma that somehow in earlier battles, the North Midland Division had not performed quite as it should.

Notes

1. J.Ewing, *The Royal Scots* Vol.II p.702

2. Like many of the 46th Division killed before crossing the canal, several of the fatalities in the attacks on Sequehart were later reinterred in Cerisy-Gailly Military Cemetery. These include Captain Francis Brain and Lieutenant Edward Boileau of the 1/Dorset and Second Lieutenant Davidson Smith, 4th attached 5/6 Royal Scots.

3. *OH 1918* Vol.V p.141

4. Bean, op.cit. Vol.VI p.1015

5. Bernard Vann VC was apparently once described by General Allenby as 'the most fearless officer I have ever met'.

6. Lieutenant-Colonel White of the 5/S.Stafford recorded: 'What was most satisfactory...was the fighting spirit of all ranks. Platoons and company commanders went for the Germans every time. This led them off their objectives sometimes, but each company had a charge to its credit and 25% of the men actually used their bayonets'. War Diary of 5/South Stafford, op.cit.

7. Lance-Corporal W.Coltman, DCM, MM of the 5/N.Stafford was awarded the VC for his bravery in several times bringing in wounded from exposed positions on the hill. Captain Charlton of Riqueval bridge fame, also again distinguished himself during the fighting and was awarded the MC.

8. L.de Grave, op.cit. p.193

9. Between 28 September and 3 October 1918 the battalion lost 80 dead. On 13 October 1915 it had 87 killed near the Hohenzollern redoubt, while at Gommecourt on 1 July 1916 it lost 162 killed. Those who died of wounds outside of those dates have been ignored.

10. War Diary of 5/Leicester. WO.95.2690

11. War Diary of 5/South Stafford. WO.95.2686

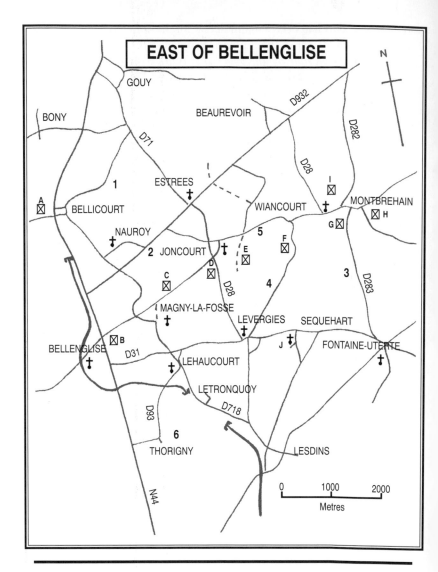

EAST OF BELLENGLISE

N

GOUY

BONY

BEAUREVOIR

D932

D282

D71

1

ESTREES

D28

I ⊠

A ⊠

BELLICOURT

WIANCOURT ✝

MONTBREHAIN ⊠ H

NAUROY ✝

2 JONCOURT ✝

5

G ⊠

E ⊠

F ⊠

C ⊠

D ⊠

D28

4

3

D283

MAGNY-LA-FOSSE ✝

LEVERGIES ✝

SEQUEHART

BELLENGLISE ✝

⊠ B

D31

LEHAUCOURT ✝

J ✝

FONTAINE-UTERTE ✝

LETRONQUOY

D93

D718

6

THORIGNY

LESDINS

N44

0   1000   2000
Metres

Key to Cemeteries

A	BELLINGLISE BRITISH	F	RAMICOURT BRITISH
B	LA BARAQUE	G	MONTBREHAIN BRITISH
C	UPLANDS	H	HIGH TREES
D	JONCOURT BRITISH	I	CALVAIRE
E	JONCOURT EAST BRITISH	J	SEQUEHART No's 1 and 2

The area today

The fields surrounding the several villages have long since returned to the plough. Trees and hedges are at a premium and the villages are undistinguished. As in all neighbouring areas a network of tracks and baulks connects the cultivated zones with the tarmac roads, thereby producing some good, easy walks for the enthusiastic visitor.

Many of the pill boxes which formed part of the Beaurevoir Line and its immediate rear still exist but are almost impossible to find in spring and summer. Built with their machine-gun slits barely above ground level, they have sunk or had earth piled around or on top of them; once the crops have sprung they disappear beneath the verdure. There are some exceptions, notably a machine-gun post not far from Joncourt British Cemetery and an observation post in th fields near the apex of the D71 and D712 to the north-west of the village. In winter the tops of several of those attacked by the 46th and 32nd Divisions north and south of the Ramicourt–Levergies road around Preselles, and those taken by the 2/Manchester east of Joncourt British Cemetery, can still be found. In the Australian sector a similar string of almost flush emplacements can be seen eiher side of the D932 about 700m east of the crossroads in Estrées.

The best way to see the area by car is probably to make several north-south sweeps using the D932 and D8 as the boundaries. These traverse the battle area running approximately parallel to the various stages of the advance. Alternatively, use the D713 and D31 to take you along rather than across the front, The gardiners of the CWGC will certainly appreciate a note in the cemetery visitors' book as calls by British travellers are infrequent.

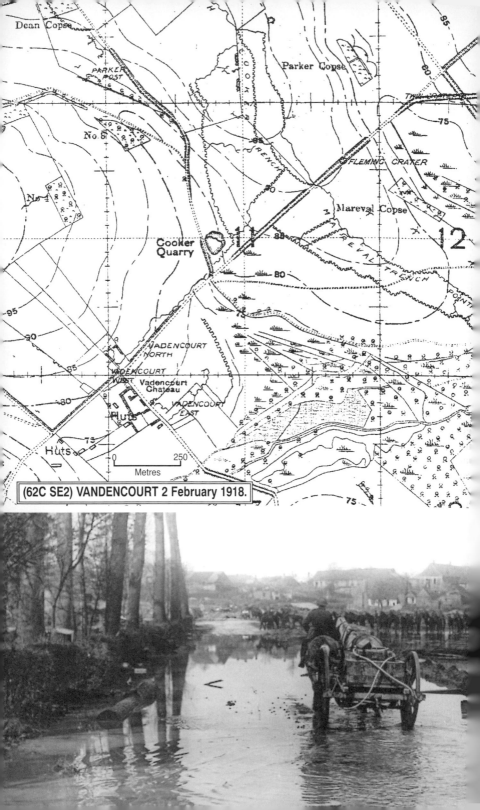

(62C SE2) VANDENCOURT 2 February 1918.

Chapter Three

VADENCOURT AND MAISSEMY

Even in its heyday, Vadencourt was never more than a chateau and a very small cluster of associated cottages. In 1918 however, its strategic importance was far greater than its physical attributes might suggest. The chateau guarded the first reliable crossing of the Omignon north of Villecholles; crossings to the south depended upon the availability of boats or, on rare occasions, a sufficiently reduced water level. The causeway from Vadencourt links the chateau with the apparently equally insignificant hamlet of Maissemy. This comprises a small collection of farms lining the main road running along the valley from Vermand. On the southern edge of the hamlet the road divides: one branch climbs up a significant ridge to the south while the other climbs a little to the east before descending towards Pontruet. In March 1918, Vadencourt and its approach through Maissemy was to play a significant part in the defence of the British Battle Zone.

In late March 1917 the 61st Division approached the Omignon Valley from the south-west. The hamlet of Marteville and the more substantial town of Vermand were found to be empty save for the occasional German cavalry patrol. During the night of 30-31 March a patrol of two officers and 20 other ranks of the 2/4 Berkshire occupied Vermand Cemetery, later using the site to bury some of their own dead. The enemy was content to allow the British to approach the Hindenburg Line but, where it suited him, paused and fought to make the advance more costly. The 2/7 Worcester pushed forward and on 1 April discovered Villecholles to be empty. Apart from the odd machine-gun team and one-man posts sited every 30m, Bihécourt too was largely deserted. On 2 April the line Bihécourt-Ponne Copse was secured and Vadencourt Chateau was found to be empty.

While their division began

British transport moving through [Vade]**ncourt in April 1917.** Although the [ro]**ads were flooded by the German** [d]**estruction of the River Cologne's** [b]**anks, the village buildings appear** [re]**markably intact.** TAYLOR LIBRARY

preparations for an attack on Maissemy and the causeway, the 2/4 Berkshire and the 2/5 Gloucester proceeded to consolidate Bihécourt. Two battalions of 183 Brigade led the assault. Concentrated small-arms fire tore into the ranks of the 2/4 and 2/6 Gloucester as they struggled up the slope to the south of Maissemy; on reaching the crest they came under yet more fire from German positions around Fresnoy-le-Petit. In contrast to this determined resistance, the Germans voluntarily abandoned a strategically sited trench on the Bihécourt-Vadencourt road, allowing the 2/7 Worcester to occupy Maissemy from the west against little opposition. It was clear that the Germans were prepared to allow the British to take any land which did not directly threaten their outpost and main line positions, but that they would fight tenaciously for any that did.

In April the 32nd Division, which had pushed north from Savy, Holnon and Gricourt, relieved the 61st, but by early May the South Midlanders were again garrisoning the sector. There was little opportunity for the British to fortify their new positions before the pressures of the Battle of Arras compelled a French division to relieve them. In due course the 59th Division and the Cavalry Corps then took over from the French. The C-in-C of the Canadian Cavalry Brigade established his HQ at Vadencourt Chateau. Another cavalry officer recalled that when his unit moved into the area, the chateau was 'nothing but a heap of bricks and mortar' and that the garden, which still showed 'traces of great expenditure in former days', displayed little of its former glory.[1] Although their surroundings were pretty miserable, Brigadier-General Seely encouraged his subordinates to raid and harass the enemy whenever circumstances permitted. Prisoners captured by the Canadians in June admitted that they had been sent to the area for a rest after their gruelling at Arras; one officer and 34 other ranks bagged in July reported that they had recently been sent down from the Messines sector.

Most of the front positions in this sector were posts rather than connected trenches. The British decided against permanently occupying Pontru because, lying in its exposed valley position, it would have been subjected to constant harassment by the Germans to the east. Posts were maintained in the hamlet, which boasted little more than a ruined sugar refinery and the walls of what once had been a dozen cottages. During the winter the positions were extended, but the principle of the British defensive strategy relied on the Battle Zone further back to absorb and halt any enemy thrusts from the direction of Pontruet and Bellenglise.

According to the *Official History*, the Battle Zone of IX Corps lay on ground

> *'very favourable for defence, a sea of low ridges and shallow*
> *depressions between the Omignon and Cologne'.*[2]

The outpost line ran back as far as Mareval and Pontru Trenches - a considerable depth - while the Battle Zone ran through Vadencourt Chateau, which was in itself a strong natural position. Officially, the Battle Zone ran from in front of Maissemy, through Vadencourt to Cooker Trench, Dean Trench and Bob Trench, to Le Verguier. The low-lying marsh which extended almost from Pontru towards Bihécourt and Villecholles meant that in this sector the enemy would have to advance either north and south of the marsh from Pontruet towards Maissemy and Le Verguier or, by approaching from the direction of Vermand to the south-east, take the Battle Zone from the rear. Despite the naturally strong defensive position, not all of the 24th Division's units were confident that enemy thrusts could be held and broken in the Vadencourt region. A report written after the battle by an officer of the 3/Rifle Brigade condemned the state of the British defences.[3] Although written with hindsight and perhaps as a justification for having withdrawn from prepared positions, the report suggests that it was 'questionable whether the defences of any position of the British line [were] ever completed'. On his battalion's sector the officer described the Red Line as being:

> *a particularly bad line...consisting of a front with no field of*
> *fire and a few dugouts...and a system of carriage drives (i.e. very*
> *broad trenches only a few feet deep which were no protection*
> *from any sort of fire)...Whoever had been organising this area*
> *for defence seems to have entirely overlooked the Golden Rule of*
> *wire first, dugouts second and trenches third.*

Battalions of 17 and 72 Brigades relieved the Cavalry Corps during the second week of March 1918. By 21 March 3/RB, the right battalion of 17 Brigade with its HQ at Caubrieres Wood Number 2, held the left sector, with the 8/West Kent on its right. The Kents' had their HQ at Vadencourt Chateau, while that of the 1/North Staffs, on the right of the Kents, was housed in the road running south from Maissemy. The forward company of the Kents had its HQ in Mustard Quarry; the remainder of the battalion was deployed principally in Mareval and Pontru Trenches. Since taking over the sector from the 2nd Dismounted Cavalry Division on 11 March, the battalion had spent ten very hard days and nights in the front line. Large patrols, sometimes of 100 men, crept over the bags nightly and, to add to the strain, some 200

March 1918

of its men were on leave in the UK.

The North Staffs relieved the 9/East Surrey during the night of 17-18 March. One company, with its HQ in Muguet Wood, held Sampson Trench; another was positioned in and around Pontruet; the third held Essling redoubt on the sector's highest ground and the fourth remained in support at Maissemy. One company of the divisional Pioneers, the 12/Sherwood Foresters in Villecholles, was earmarked to support the Staffs should the need arise. To the south of the North Staffs was the 13/Middlesex of 73 Brigade. It was informed on 20 March that the battalion would be placed under corps' orders while it held a line of four small redoubts north of the Omignon between Vermand and Bihécourt. Its battalion HQ was housed at Vermand Chateau.

The massive bombardment of gas and HE which presaged the German assault compelled Battalion HQ staffs to wear their respirators until about 10.30am. The colonels of 72 Brigade's two front battalions knew little of what was happening in their forward positions. Telephone cables had been cut and few runners successfully struggled through the bombardment. On the front of the 8/West Kent, the enemy was seen to be approaching from Maissemy and Pontru Trench. Captain Needham arrived at Vadencourt Chateau with a gaping wound and news that the front line platoons had been surprised by the sudden appearance of the enemy through the mist and that few of his company had escaped. The company managed to put up sufficient resistance to allow members of 103rd Field Company to blow the bridge over the Omignon before the Germans were across. The enemy pushed back the company of the 1/North Staffs defending Pontruet, which then allowed him to send columns of infantry down the Bellenglise-Vermand road

A French orchard deliberately destroyed by the Germans as they withdrew to the Hindenburg Line in 1917.

and over the ridge above Maissemy to the south. The Kents' HQ did not yet know that Maissemy had fallen but, when it saw enemy troops passing to the north and south of the chateau, brought down heavy frontal and enfilade fire upon them. Whole battalions of German infantry could be seen advancing across the Kents' front in the direction of Cooker Quarry. Assisted by guns of the 24th MGC, the battalion's Lewis gunners did 'tremendous execution', but calls to the artillery to bring down an bombardment on the enemy met with a disappointing response. Some of the British guns that did open fire dropped their shells short and added to the rising toll of British casualties. However, while Cooker Trench and the quarry held, the Queen's Own remained confident of preventing an enemy breakthrough down the Vermand road.

The 'black buttons' of 3/RB were also fighting hard. Telephone lines from Battalion HQ to B Company in the outpost line and C in support at Cooker Quarry were broken early. The other two companies were in reserve near Vadencourt, from where they made a difficult and bloody movement to their alarm positions near HQ during the early morning. D Company went into one of the several deep dugouts in the wood to await developments. A small number of stragglers from B Company escaped back to Cooker Quarry where Captain Fenner's company put up a 'splendid fight'.[4] It continued to delay the enemy until about 6.30pm when, with the company almost surrounded, Fenner decided to withdraw. What was left of the company fell back on Vadencourt and then Bihécourt. Fenner organised the retirement but was killed later the following day. The support companies rallied on a line just to the west of Dean Copse. They had no trenches but put up a 'great fight against immense odds'.[5] At about 7.00pm a runner from Fenner's company arrived at Battalion announcing that the quarry had fallen and that the Germans were penetrating between Dean Copse and Le Verguier. HQ immediately requested reinforcements. These arrived in the shape of a squadron of 5th Dragoon Guards and one company each of the 1/RF and 12/SF. Their arrival did little to halt the enemy surge and during the night HQ of 3/RB fell back to Brigade HQ at Small Foot Wood. This became the rallying point for battalion stragglers.

The final attack on the quarry was witnessed by troops of the 8/West Kent defending their position at the chateau. With the retreat of the RB from Cooker Quarry and the news that the enemy was through to the south, the Queen's flanks were in the air. The enemy was pouring up Watling Street and firing a trench mortar at the crossroads just north of the chateau. The colonel decided the battalion would have to adhere to the general withdrawal and, leaving a rearguard of four Vickers and four Lewis at the chateau (most of their teams eventually rejoined the battalion), retired towards Vermand.

Among the less familiar units which fought with the 24th Division during this period were the 19th Entrenching Battalion and the 11/Hussars. The entrenching battalion had been created in February from 450 men of the disbanded 10/Royal Dublin Fusiliers and 200 from the 7/Leinster. It had no official Lewis gun section, signallers or stretcher bearers and was put into the line south of the Omignon to support B Squadron of the 11/Hussars. The Prince Albert's Own had been moved up as counter-attack troops for 74 Brigade and were warned they would be required to move against the enemy once the high ground on their right had been won back by the 2/4 Berkshire. The redoubtable Lieutenant-Colonel Dimmer VC led two companies against the enemy south of Maissemy. According to one officer, Dimmer was a 'great believer in moral effect'[6] and consequently elected to lead the attack mounted. Accompanied by his groom, they advanced against the enemy whom they encountered in 'overwhelming numbers'.[7] Dimmer fell, and the survivors of the two companies withdrew. The supportive attack by the Hussars was cancelled, their colonel instead being ordered to take command of all 74 Brigade troops south of the river. Besides his own regiment Colonel Anderson's command consisted of three companies from each of the 9/East Surrey, 19th Entrenching Battalion and 12/SF and about three officers and 25 men from the 1/North Staffs. Their task was to prevent a German advance down the south bank of the river or the high ground to its south.

With the marsh on its left, a party of the Surreys manned a post on the Villecholles-Maissemy road. To the right, C Squadron of the Hussars and some more Surreys held Mount Huette Wood, supported by a company of the Pioneers. The Foresters were sheltering in a sunken lane which ran down the hill to Villecholles. On the right of the wood and running up the slope to the site of Villecholles mill was Spooner redoubt. Although this position was well wired, its trenches were only about two feet deep. However, with its left held by A Squadron of the Hussars and some East Surreys, and on its right by companies of the 1/8 Argyll & Sutherland Highlanders, it commanded good fields of fire and observation over the enemy's potential approaches.

Once again protected by an enveloping mist, the Germans attacked

Spooner redoubt in the early hours of 22 March. Scores were mown down as they struggled to get through the British wire. Inside the perimeter, Major Moir of the Argylls calmly walked up and down the defences, encouraging and exhorting his men. In the valley below, the Germans dribbled past the Surreys' post on the Villecholles road, thus bringing the troops in Mount Huette Wood under enfilade from the left rear. Furthermore, when the mist cleared at around 10.00am, Spooner itself came under fire from the right rear. Enemy machine guns were already firing into Vermand from Bihécourt; if the Germans penetrated any further down the Holnon–Vermand road, the redoubt would be virtually cut off. At his HQ in Vermand, Colonel Anderson was aware of the deteriorating situation and at mid-day sent a runner to the redoubt instructing the defenders to withdraw. A two feet deep communication trench ran back from Mount Huette Wood up to the redoubt and on to the sunken lane behind. Men from the wood and Spooner crowded into the trench which, enfiladed from close range, rapidly became choked with dead and wounded. Panic was about to erupt and, with the Germans close behind, disaster loomed. Scores of troops herded towards the only gap in the British wire. An enemy machine gun was already playing on the gap and, to add to the general chaos, low-flying aircraft strafed the communication trench and its surrounds. Amidst the pandemonium Major Moir's stentorian voice bellowed out: 'Stand fast the Argylls'. Other officers immediately joined in and men began to collect around them. Several parties laid down and opened fire on the advancing Germans; order was gradually brought to the clogged route of retreat. Another company of the 19th Entrenching Battalion came up to form a more organised rearguard, and under its cover the defenders of Spooner and Mount Huette Wood withdrew through Vermand.

Following closely upon the heels of 74 Brigade, the enemy pressed home his advantage. He was brought to a temporary halt by the 50th Division manning the Green Line west of Vermand. On the right of 74 Brigade, battalions of the Argylls' division, the 61st, withdrew on Holnon Wood.

The Germans believed that if momentum could be maintained, once they were through the Battle Zone there would be little to stop them until Péronne. The 24th Division had fought hard for its sector and had inflicted heavy losses on the Germans; the number of graves with dates of 21 or 22 March in Maissemy German Cemetery bears witness to that. The 24th's divisional commander, Major-General Daly, issued an emotional 'thank you' to the survivors. He mentioned the Hussars and the 19th Entrenching Battalion for their 'very gallant rearguard' and after declaring that every man of the division was 'a hero', finished by stating that the division remained 'intact, defiant and unbroken'.(8) A message from 17 Brigade HQ two weeks after the onslaught reiterated the GOC's comments. The Brigadier thought that 'no more adverse conditions for a successful defence could be imagined'. He stressed how the brigade's system of defence in depth and mutually supporting fire had been jeopardised by the mist. 'It was', he said,

> *only by personal gallantry and good leadership, assisted by the fog, that the brigade got out at all'.*[9]

September 1918 Fog again shrouded the banks of the Omignon on the morning of 18 September. A wet, dank dawn made visual signalling between battalions of 2 Brigade impossible and direction keeping difficult. The 2/Sussex jumped off either side of the Bellenglise-Vermand road, just to the west of where Vadencourt British Cemetery now stands. The Sussex had Australians on their left and the 2/KRRC across the marsh on their right. The Sussex were to pass over Cooker Quarry, take the old British lines of Cooker, Mareval and Pontru Trenches and thus secure the high ground overlooking Pontru. The Rifles, with the 1/Cameron Highlanders on their right, were to advance astride the Maissemy–Berthaucourt road and then, by dropping down into Berthaucourt itself, link up with the Sussex. The attack was a success. The Sussex cleared Mustard Quarry, where they took a large number of prisoners, and advanced towards the tumulus and Ste Hélène. Two officers were later singled out for showing especially good leadership: Captain Dolleymore of the Sussex and Second Lieutenant Cunningham of the Rifles, who died of wounds the following day. The going had been hard but Dominion and British troops were now almost within sight of the Hindenburg outpost line. There remained several nasty obstacles to be overcome and bitter engagements to be fought before the assault against the line itself could begin. But, the approaches had been won, and preparations duly began.

Notes

1. F.Whitmore, *The 10th PWO Royal Hussars and Essex Yeomanry during the European War*, p.138
2. *Official History 1918*, Vol.I p.187
3. War Diary of 3/RB. WO.95.2206
4. Ibid
5. Ibid
6. Letter written by Captain A.Whitfield appended to War Diary of 2/4 Berks. WO.95.3065
7. Ibid
8. Message from Major-General A.Daly, 3 April 1918, appended to War Diary of 3/RB.
9. Message from 17 Brigade, 10 April 1918, appended to War Diary of 3/RB.

Vadencourt Today

It is almost an exaggeration to describe Vadencourt as a hamlet. Its chateau was rebuilt and stands again north of the causeway over the Omignon. It boasts a few trout ponds within its grounds and exudes an air of prosperity. A handful of lesser dwellings line the same road the junction of the D33. Six hundred metres east of the junction is Cooker Quarry. Tucked on the reverse slope, the quarry retains nothing of its wartime significance save for the odd piece of ordnance. Caubrieres Woods to the north are private property and appear not to have any evidence of the large dugouts which once punctured their soils. Three hundred metres from the quarry along the D33 is Maissemy German Cemetery. Vadencourt British Cemetery lies 600m in the opposite direction.

Although there is not much to Bihécourt, it is worth a visit. A short drive past the farms on its southern road ends at the flooded valley of the Omignon. The difficulties faced by the Germans on 21 March can be easily appreciated. Today it is a tranquil scene of aquatic charm, the quiet punctuated only by the chattering of ducks and geese. To the north of the village crossroads, an unmade road leads up a hill before descending into a sheltered valley which once contained Ponne Copse. Until March 1918 this was the site of billeting huts; in October of that year, several CCSs established themselves within its folds.

Traffic on the N29 passes to the north of Vermand. The town, which possesses a church with a rather bizarre steeple and a museum of the area, is built on something of a slope. The sole advantage of the steeple is that it can be seen from a considerable distance and thus provides a useful sighting point. There is a memorial to one of the town's sons killed in a recent colonial war and another to a soldier of the Free French Forces killed near the quarries in September 1944. The communal cemetery, reached at the end of a gravel road, is on the west side of the town.

Villecholles is a line of pleasant town housing fronting the road from Maissemy. The road joins the N29 south of the old railway line which marked the first crossing of the Omignon beyond Maissemy. Modern housing continues along the Rue de la Tour at the village crossroads. The road climbs and soon becomes a track. This forks at the site of Spooner redoubt. Today, the open field belies its violent past. Mount Huette Wood has disappeared but a recent civilian cemetery now sits beside the road 400m on from where the wood once hid men of the Hussars and East Surreys.

Maissemy has a village green and some well-kept large farms. The churchyard has reverted to a natural state, overgrown and neglected. Fallen gravestones hidden beneath the grass and brambles trip the unwary visitor. Five British burials from the 35th Division were removed from the churchyard to Vadencourt some time after the war. The village war memorial has an unusual coloured plaque. Besides the names of those who fell in the two world wars, five members of the Jaskorski family who were killed in May 1940 at Crèvecoeur-le-Grand are commemorated. The picturesque D735 runs north to cross the causeway to Vadencourt; the D73 goes east and in just over one mile passes Berthaucourt Communal Cemetery. The D735 continues on to join the N29 west of Holnon.

Tour of Vadencourt
(Tour Map 2)
13.5kms, 8.5miles. 3.25 hours

Park at Vadencourt British Cemetery and walk south along the D33 to Bihécourt. Turn left at the crossroads in the village to the flooded Omignon valley. Retrace your steps and go straight over at the crossroads onto a gravel road. 1400m along several tracks converge in the valley bottom. Take the right fork. This climbs up past Small Foot

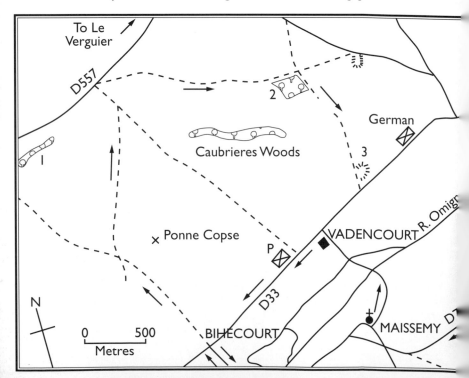

Vadencourt British Cemetery is not one of the most attractive in the area, but it does contain a number of interesting graves. About one fifth of the total are those of unidentified soldiers.

Wood. **(1)** At 1600m the track meets another at a T-junction. Turn left and after 350m it joins the D577. Turn right onto the road (towards Le Verguier) and after 200m the road bends to the left. Take the right fork. This track slopes gently south of Le Verguier and comes to Dean Copse after 2000m. **(2)** Caubrieres Woods are to your right. Walk down the east face of Dean Copse. The headland vanishes, but go straight on, keeping to the edge of the field. After 200m you again pick up a track. Follow this down to Cooker Quarry **(3)** and rejoin the D33. Turn left and walk up to the German cemetery.

Continue down the slope of the D33 and turn right to Pontru at the crossroads. Mustard Quarry was in the field behind the farm north of the road. **(4)** Walk through the village and on into what used to be Berthaucourt. Turn right at the crucifix onto the D73. Berthaucourt Communal Cemetery is on the left. Keep on this road to reach

Cooker Quarry from the Vadencourt road. Well positioned on the reverse slope, Cooker Trench ran away to the left and Mareval Trench to the right. The position of the German cemetery is marked by the trees on the right.

Although it has the usual air of melancholy, Maissemy is one of the brighter German cemeteries. The dull red sandstone walls and entrance are lightened by the central building and well-spaced trees.

Maissemy. Turn right by the church and follow the road across the causeway. Vadencourt Chateau is on your left. At the junction, turn left onto the D33 and walk 200m to your car.

Tour of Maissemy
(Tour Map 3)
(6.7kms, 4miles. 1.5 hours)

Park on the verge by Maissemy church. Walk along the D73 towards Vermand. Just after the communal cemetery **(1)** (900m from Maissemy) take the track to the left. This passes the new quarry and curls around to join the D735. Turn right and climb up the hill until a crucifix between two trees is reached. There are excellent views across to Fresnoy and Gricourt. Take the track opposite the crucifix. This eventually drops down to Otter Copse and Holnon, but turn left after 600m. This track turns 90-degrees left after 400m towards a copse. **(2)** There are more good views across to Essling redoubt **(3)** (water tower) and the high ground east of the canal. There is a 90-degree right turn in front of the copse. Follow the track down into the valley. British communication trenches crossed this ground on their way to Essling redoubt and Sampson Trench. At a crossing of tracks, either turn left for the shorter route back to Maissemy or straight over to join the D73 between Maissemy and Pontru. (The right track used to follow the valley to Arbousiers Wood **(4)** and Cornouillers Valley. Today it has been ploughed out in one section and is too overgrown in another). Where the track joins the D73, turn left to turn to Maissemy.

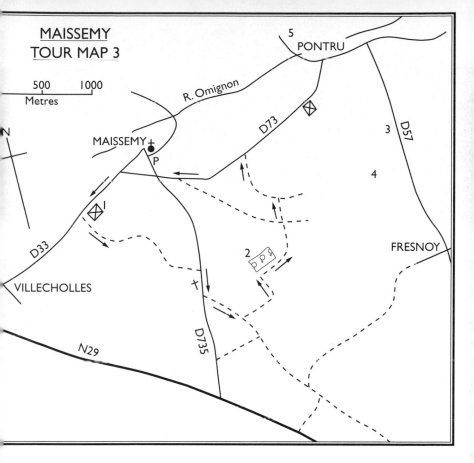

A visit to Spooner Redoubt

A walk up to the site of the redoubt from the centre of Villecholles is worth the effort. Unfortunately, the tracks which go past the site are only for access to fields on the crest or down to the N29 to the south. Park on the *Rue de la Tour* near the chapel at the crossroads of the D73 and walk up the hill. The road becomes a track. Fork left up to the summit. The fork to the right leads to the quarries east of Vermand.

British Tommies and French poilu enjoy a rest and a smoke in reserve
trenches near Le Verguier in April 1917.

Chapter Four

LE VERGUIER AND ASCENSION VALLEY

Dominating the ground to its west, south and east, the small village of Le Verguier sits on top of a hill overlooking the Omignon Valley. To the south, the river meanders its leisurely way to its confluence with the Somme, while fairly sharp slopes descend to Jeancourt in the west and the Hargicourt–Pontru road to the east. On top of the opposite ridge stands Grand Priel Farm. As the Germans retreated towards the Hindenburg Line in March 1917, it soon became apparent that one of the several positions on which they would stand and fight was Le Verguier.

Three British Territorial divisions fought side by side in this sector during the German retreat. The middle one of the three was the least experienced. The 59th (2/North Midland) was sandwiched between the two South Midland Divisions, the 48th to the north and the 61st to the south. Like most of the second line Territorial divisions, the 59th had only arrived in France earlier that year. Since then it had spent most of its time following the German withdrawal and building roads. At Le Verguier 178 Brigade faced its first real test.

The Sherwood Foresters Brigade was delegated the task of taking the formidable German positions within the village. The ruins bristled with strongpoints which enjoyed excellent fields of fire down the slopes. Thick wire entanglements were strewn across the probable

The remains of Fort Bell in Le Verguier, September 1918. The position was the scene of ferocious defence by the 8/Queen's in March and by German units in September. When it fell, the Australians captured over 50 men from its ruins.

Le Verguier from the Jeancourt road, with Pieumel Wood on the left. In April 1917 one company of the 2/7 Sherwood Foresters attempted to advance up the hill from this direction, and was bloodily repulsed.

approaches, all of which had been accurately registered by the German artillery to the rear. The Foresters made several attempts to climb and hack their way through into the ruins, but on each occasion were bloodily repulsed. Thick snow further hampered their efforts and the over-optimism of the divisional artillery in expecting that a short bombardment would deal with the wire, doomed the brigade to costly failure. The 2/7 SF had been the first to try on 2 April. One company was to advance up the hill from Jeancourt, while the rest of the battalion approached the village along the main spur from Vendelles. When the attack began, the company moving up from Jeancourt was almost annihilated; the others were baulked by the intensity of the enemy's fire. The 2/5 Battalion tried next and met with a similar result. The 2/8th was the last battalion to make the attempt. The surviving troops were reported to be 'very despondent'[1] at having failed in their first attack, but it was a task which would have tested the most experienced of soldiers. The brigade's new GOC later expressed his doubts about the wisdom of the operation but, because he did not officially take command until after the attack, he had refrained from referring his reservations to Division. Four days later, when the 61st Division had won its way to the top of the ridge which stands above Maissemy and Berthaucourt, the enemy voluntarily relinquished the rubble of Le Verguier and withdrew to the north and east.

Once in occupation, the 59th Division began to fortify the position. Battalions usually spent about one week in the village and its nearby front line posts. However, as it was over 2000m behind the forward positions and protected by Ascension Ridge to the east, the village's western slopes were used for billeting. Consequently, the tumbled ruins often became the target for German artillery. In March 1918 it formed part of the 24th Division's Battle Zone, in which several strongpoints - Fort Greathead and Fort Bell for example - were designed to break up the anticipated rushes of German infantry should they penetrate beyond the Forward Zone. The 24th Division had side-stepped a little south from the Hargicourt sector in late February and took over the area from the 2nd Dismounted Cavalry Division in early March.

By that time, the first early verdant shoots of spring were struggling to make an appearance amid the shelled ruins of the village. Lt Wilfred Grout of the 1/RF remembered that:

Spring of 1918 came in like a lamb; the first daylight hours were fresh and beautiful. I wrote my diary seated in the garden of our billet in Le Verguier, my back resting against a tree trunk and by my side the satchel containing my gas mask. We had an abundance of unpruned currant and gooseberry bushes, strawberry beds overgrown with grass and nettles; a plantation of fir trees eight feet high; flowering bushes in profusion. All the fruit trees had been lopped off at the bole and pruned viciously; a vegetable garden hidden under a fallen tree and a tangle of barbed wire; snowdrops, violets and daffodils. Romantic and peaceful, but there was something sinister about the atmosphere.[2]

During the night of 18-19 March the 8/Queen's (Royal West Surrey) relieved the 1/Royal Fusiliers in and around the village. Two companies went into the Forward Zone outposts, with company HQs at Shepherd's Copse and Graham's Post. The other two were deployed within the village. The following night, A Company's HQ was moved back from Graham's Post to Grand Priel Crater. These were the positions held during the initial stages of the German bombardment on 21 March. Battalion HQ seized the opportunity of a temporary lull in the shelling later in the day to transfer from its original position a little south of Fort Greathead to a sunken road south-west of the village. Just managing to avoid capture by the German penetration down the valley from Villeret, A Company's HQ was also shifted in the nick of time. It took up residence in Orchard Post. By the time Battalion HQ discovered the attack had actually begun, most men of the forward companies were either dead or captured.

Platoons were distributed throughout eight posts within the village and its immediate surrounds. The majority of these held on for most of the offensive's opening day. The enemy, frustrated by Lewis-gun fire and the wire, reverted to bombarding the positions during the night. Enemy infantry were through to the north and south and by 6.30am on 22 March all the defended areas, with the exception of Forts Lees and Greathead, were surrounded. Shortly after, Battalion HQ was attacked but the details managed to drive off the enemy. Fort Lees was finally overcome at 9.30am and, with the acute danger of complete envelopment, the garrison of Fort Greathead and HQ details assembled in the sunken road preparatory to withdrawal. Covered by a Lewis-gun team, the Surreys fell back through the mist and joined their comrades of 17 Brigade, the 1/RF, on the ridge to the west of Vendelles.

In the end Le Verguier had fallen to overwhelming odds from three sides. The 8/Queen's had suffered grievous losses during the two day battle, managing to muster only 11 officers and 150 other ranks at Montecourt on 23 March. However, its resolute defence of the village was immediately acknowledged. *The Times* of 26 March praised the battalion's stand, and the 24th Division as a whole was the first division to be singled out for mention in official dispatches.

In view of its commanding position, the village was again expected

Australians of the 45th Battalion beginning to dig in on their objective in Ascension Valley, 18 September 1918. A smoke and high explosive barrage falls on the opposite slope. An officer of the 8/Sherwood Foresters recalled that the valley was 'never a place to linger in, as most nights and early mornings the Hun was in the habit of treating it liberally with high explosive and gas shells'. IWM E3247

Ascension Valley today is far removed from the frantic scenes it witnessed as the 46th Division moved into its gentle folds in preparation for the attack on the canal. For much of 1917 the valley was No Man's Land, coming to life after dark when patrols criss-crossed its fields. Somerville Wood is left, Red Wood above Angle Bank centre and the trees of Ascension Farm above right. The dark mass of trees beyond is Grand Priel Woods.

to provide its defenders of September 1918 with advantages over British and Dominion troops approaching it from the west. The enemy was expected to have strongly reinforced and realigned the original British defences and to make a determined stand within them; he would then make a staged withdrawal to the former British Forward Zone and outpost line. Behind those, and across what had been No Man's Land of March, lay the outpost positions of the Hindenburg

September 1918

Line. It was to the Australian 4th Division that the task of assaulting the village fell. Despite discovering wire in the sunken roads leading to the village, the 16th Battalion, with two other battalions of 4 Brigade passing to the north and south, cleared the ruins with surprisingly little resistance. The only really prolonged stands were made by defenders in Fort Bell and Fort Lees. With the fall of the village and the woods to its north, the Australians pressed on to Ascension Ridge. Fresh troops, followed by batteries of howitzers, flowed into Le Verguier. The site became an assembly area for units preparing to attack the Hindenburg Line. Already a 'most unpleasant and smelly place',[3] one deep dugout used as a battalion HQ in a quarry just to the north of the village was made worse by batteries of 8-inch howitzers and 60-pounders arriving in the road behind.

April 1917

When the 59th Division took Grand Priel and Ascension Farms on 13-14 April 1917, there remained some substantial standing walls and cellars on both sites. This was just as well for their new occupants, the 2/6 North Staffs. Enemy artillery regularly bracketed the positions for several days after their capture. During the course of the summer, German guns destroyed most of what had remain intact above ground, but the subterranean passages were converted into company and battery HQ. Both farms had observation over Ascension Valley and over sections of the Hindenburg outpost line. Posts were established to the north and south of both farms and were taken over and extended by units of the 35th Division and by Indian and Canadian cavalry. The 23/Manchester established a post at Lone Tree, and on 5 May a party of six officers and 189 other ranks captured the wood to its north; this was immediately dubbed Somerville Wood after the officer who led the assault. An earlier attempt to take the wood by the Staffordshire Brigade of the 59th Division had failed, as did a subsequent attack by the 20/LF. A patrol of the Fusiliers hurriedly withdrew having stirred up what a diarist described as a 'hornets nest.'[4]

A large crater to the west of Ste Hélène was also named after another officer of the 23rd, Captain Fisher. Many posts, christened with animal or human names, were dug into the reverse or western slopes of Ascension Spur. One such dugout behind Red Wood was known as Hodson's Post. It was probably named after Captain Hodson of the 15/Cheshire rather than in honour of the 9th Hodson's Horse which also spent some time in the sector. In later months, following some typographical or cartographical error, it became known more commonly as Hudson Post. By March 1918 several of these posts had grown into substantial constructions with layers of sandbags and loop holes facing every direction. Lone Tree Post was developed into a series of trenches and dugouts protected by quantities of concertina wire. As he waited with his platoon in the improvised trenches between Le Verguier and Vendelles throughout 21 March, Lieutenant Wilfred Grout's thoughts went out to the men in the forwards posts:

> 'There was no hope for the men in Lone Tree Post, and maybe in Graham Post was being enacted the real tragedy of Journey's End'.[5]

Battalions in the line spent a great many nocturnal hours patrolling Ascension Valley. Parties of 20 and more from the 1/RF regularly investigated Ascension Wood and the area in front of Buisson-Gaulaine Farm. Two subalterns of the 12/RF, Hills and Mears-Devenish, received a note of commendation from their divisional general for having spent 'most of [their] time in No Man's Land'.[6] Their activities were usually concentrated in and around Somerville Wood and Angle Bank. The 1/RF sent out patrols twice nightly through Somerville Wood and rarely came upon any Germans. It came as something of a surprise therefore when two officers were killed on the same night by a sniper hiding among the still leafy trees.

The Canadians of the Cavalry Brigade were prodigious raiders. During their occupation of the area it was unusual if nocturnal patrols did not go out and explore the valley. Lieutenant Harvey VC frequently led patrols of Strathcona's Horse into Big and Little Bill and Ascension Wood. There was not much to the wood, much as it is today, a collection of saplings and brush with little undergrowth, but on one visit the Canadians discovered five dead Indians of the 20/Deccan Horse and a German corpse in a bad state of decomposition. The party buried the remains and continued its patrol. On another occasion Lieutenant Tatlow led a successful raid on Fisher Crater and the ruins of Ste Hélène beyond. There was a single casualty,

> 'One man killed (treacherously). Corporal – who captured two prisoners and was shot by one whilst disarming the other'.[7]

The Canadians frequently visited the crater and the nearby ruins because they were a favourite haunt of enemy snipers. One diary entry recorded the activities of a sniper but dismissed the inherent danger by

German troops surrendering to Australians in Ascension Valley, 18 September 1918.

The German strongpoint of Coronet Post. The vague ruins of Ascension Farm can be seen in the distance. IWM E3246

contemptuously deciding that 'his shooting was rotten'.[8]

Other regiments also showed a keen interest in the trenches near Ste Hélène. Members of 1 Cavalry Brigade undertook a major raid on the night of 9-10 March 1918 against Eleven Trees and Square Copse. Troopers of the Bays and 11/Hussars left Lone Tree Post and advanced across No Man's Land to Angle Bank where they regrouped. They captured two men of the recently arrived *25th Infantry Regiment, 208th Division* at Eleven Trees, but the next stage of the operation, to penetrate Square Copse, was frustrated when the Bangalore torpedo was knocked out. With the Germans fully awake to their intent, the raiders withdrew, taking some of their 11 dead and 30 wounded with them.

A prominent physical feature of the area is the ancient tumulus on the south end of Ascension Spur, 300m from Somerville Wood. The mound was occupied and then abandoned by the 2/4 Berkshire on 9 April 1917; Corporal Preston prudently withdrew his section when in danger of being surrounded by almost 200 Germans. Another patrol the following day discovered that it was again unoccupied so a temporary post was established by the 19/DLI. During the Canadian stint in the area it was known as Seely's Tumulus after the C-in-C of the Canadian Cavalry Brigade.When the German attack on Vadencourt was under way eleven days after the big raid by the Bays and Hussars, enemy artillery spotters on the mound could be clearly seen reporting by telephone on the fall of shot around Cooker Quarry. From the British point of view it was a pity that artillery could not be brought to bear on the road running beneath the tumulus. All day long German transport queued while waiting for the infantry to get through Le Verguier and Vadencourt. Unfortunately, British retaliation was described as 'very thin'[9] all day and this magnificent target remained unmolested.

September 1918 When Australians of the 45th Battalion crested Ascension Spur on 18 September 1918, they anticipated coming under immediate fire from the tumulus and Ste Hélène Ridge to the east. Fortunately the fire

Taken from where Orchard Trench crossed the Le Verguier–Hargicourt road, this photo looks south-east. The trees of Mill Spinney are on the right, Red Wood on the crest above, Collins Copse centre and the copse which now marks the former site of Ascension Farm, left.

was sporadic and, in conjunction with the 48th Battalion, they extended down the spur to capture several German guns. The 13th Battalion took the sites of several other ruined farms, once again meeting uneven resistance. Despite an armament of a dozen machine guns, the garrison of Coronet Post skulked below in its extensive dugout until capture. Another 80 Germans were captured near Ascension Farm, and at Priel Crater a German battalion HQ surrendered without a fight. The Australians were now in sight of the wire and parapets of the Hindenburg outpost line and of the mêlée of horse teams in Ascension Valley frantically hauling away gun batteries.

Coming under concerted fire from snipers and machine guns in the outpost line, some Australians began to dig in on the eastern slope of the spur. Firing Lewis guns from the hip, others, notably the 14th Battalion, kept going and advanced into the valley. Harassed by fire from Ascension Wood and Big and Little Bill, they reached the bank of the road which followed the line of the Buisson and Ste Hélène Ridges. To their south, having cleared Pontru, the 2/Sussex and 2/KRRC were trying to get to the tumulus. The Sussex achieved some progress but the Rifles had been badly held up in Berthaucourt. By the time the two British battalions made contact, the Australians were again on the move. The Sussex were ordered to conform and attack at midnight with the objective of securing a footing in the sunken road passing through Ste Hélène. As a consequence of the short notice and the heavy casualties sustained earlier in the day, the attack was largely unsuccessful. One platoon did get to the road north of the hamlet, but B Company could not get beyond Formi Trench. By dawn a right flank had been thrown back to link with the KRRs near Berthaucourt. To their north, the Australians had been more successful. During the night the 46th Battalion attacked across the valley to reinforce the 14th's tenuous grip on the road bank. Clearing the bank, and with the Germans in apparent disarray, the Australians advanced through Square Copse. Numerous dugouts were cleared and the ground won consolidated; by 20 September the whole valley and the outpost line was under British and Dominion control.

It had been a remarkable advance. Several Australian battalions were so under-strength that they had attacked with fewer than 100 rifles. This weakness was a consequence of the failure of sufficient drafts from Australia and of the sudden departure on home leave of several hundred men who had last seen their homeland in 1915. Since the launching of the Allied counter-attack on 8 August, the ANZAC Corps had regularly been in the forefront of the fighting and had suffered accordingly. The belief that its troops were being asked to do too much was one cause of the 1st Battalion's refusal at Hargicourt to go back into the line.

Having reached the Hindenburg outpost line the Australians were now within distant sight of the great squat bulk of St Quentin cathedral and of the murky water of the canal in the valley beneath. The tired and hugely depleted Dominion brigades were relieved by the 46th Division. The North Midlanders used a lull in the fighting to make preparations for their attack on the canal and the Hindenburg Line. The division occupied Ascension Valley, utilising recent German positions and former British dugouts on the western slopes of the spur as command posts and shelters. The valley and its western slopes soon became a thronging mass of humanity and material. Brigades marched in as others marched out, field gun batteries were dug in and the heavier guns trundled and hauled into position behind them. Grand Priel Farm became the RFA Group HQ, with the batteries of 231 Brigade RFA dispersed around it. Hodson's Post served as battalion HQ for, among others, the 5/Leicester and 6/South Staffs. Three brigade HQs were scattered around Red Wood and Ascension Wood, while several Aid Posts were established near the tumulus and in Cooker Quarry. 46th Bn MGC had its companies dug in near Eleven Trees, Victoria Crossroads and Little Bill, while 230 Brigade RFA had its batteries at Graham's Post and elsewhere. The 1/Monmouth, Pioneers to the division, worked on tracks immediately behind the front positions; its Battalion HQ was sited just to the south of Square Copse.

With the guns massed and the men assembled, preparations were complete. The 46th Division's attack against Bellenglise and the canal was an outstanding success. Men and guns once again moved forward. However, the three roads which ran across Ascension Spur and Buisson Ridge remained essential arteries of the British advance; the valley once more became an area for troops out on rest and for dumps of the plethora of war.

Notes

1. *The 59th Division 1915-1918*, (various authors) p.51
2. W. Grout, quoted in *The Kaiser's War*, ed. by E.Cawston
3. War Diary of *5/Leicester, 26 September 1918.* WO.95.2690
4. H.Davson, *The 35th Division in the Great War,* p.108
5. Grout, op.cit
6. War Diary of 12/Royal Fusiliers. WO.95.2208
7. War Diary of Lord Strathcona's Horse. WO.95.1085
8. Ibid
9. War Diary of 8/West Kent. WO.95.2213

As well as its own dead, Le Verguier's war memorial also acknowledges the 24th Division's defence of the village in March 1918.

Le Verguier and Ascension Valley today

Much like most of the other villages in the area, Le Verguier has little to particularly recommend it other than an unusual war memorial. Sited in front of the church gates, it has a coloured relief of a poilu and a commemoration to the British 24th Division. It is a working village, a little beyond the normal commuter distance to St Quentin. It has a quiet air of industry and today offers the rare sight of timber seasoning naturally alongside the wares of a monumental stonemason. The water tower could do with a coat of paint and the church is singularly uninteresting. There are two Australians and one man from the 5/Border, all of whom died in September 1918, buried in the churchyard. There is a terrace of a dozen almost Zola-like workmen's

See map page 66

cottages in *Rue de la Cité* **(1)** and a path at the end of the row leads down to the *Rue de Ladessous* **(2)**. This was the sunken lane which temporarily housed the HQ of the 8/Queen's during the German offensive. The quarry to the north of the village which often served as HQ to line-holding units is now just a depression in the field west of Pieumel Wood **(3)**. Fort Bell, 200m to its south, was in the enclosed area on the reverse slope **(4)**. A few straggling trees and bushes now occupy the site.

75

After the war, surviving members of the 24th Division paid for the rebuilding of the church belfry. In recognition of the stand made by them and their fallen comrades, the village named a road after the division.

The several copses on the valley slope to the east of the village have regrown very much in the same shapes and places. Heart Copse **(5)**, Mill Spinney **(6)** and Faggot Wood **(7)** are easily identified, as is Collins Copse and its quarry on the other side of the D57**(8)**. Further north, almost opposite where the road from the 'chateau' in Grand Priel Woods joins the D57, Shepherds' Copse **(9)** retains its still significant bank. A recent quarry has disfigured its northern face; a quarry known as Harrods Stores a little to the north has been filled in. The rectangular shape of Cottage Copse is a few metres higher up the hill towards Villeret.

Grand Priel Farm is a substantial enclave of workers' cottages and farm buildings. The cottages are quite well maintained but the farm's principal outbuildings further east are dilapidated. The visitor is warned against walking through the courtyard to the track beyond. The lane down to Ascension Valley and the valley itself bear no reminders of the bustle and activity which once characterised its sloping sides. Big and Little Bill **(10 & 11)** have regrown and Ascension Wood **(12)** is there, albeit in something of a bedraggled state. The distant hum of motorway traffic is just audible above the twittering of the larks. The fields are planted and the woods gentle. It is a place of tranquillity and peace.

Ascension Farm is no more **(13)**. Its commanding position over the valley is now partly covered by trees. There are several lumps of concrete scattered about the trees, but they probably date from a later period. Again, there is little to to help the mind imagine the ferocity witnessed by its cellars and dugouts in 1917 and 1918. Somerville **(14)**

The ruins of Ascension Farm after their capture, September 1918. IWM E3252

The sunken lane on the left is *Rue de Ladessous*. A dugout in this lane became the HQ of the 8/Queen's during 21 March 1918. The barn (centre) and its accompanying buildings mark the site of Fort Greathead.

and Red Woods **(15)** can be seen along the crest to the south and Angle Bank **(16)** cuts into the valley slope below. Further down the spur, a circle of trees marks the still significant mound of the tumulus.

Tour of Le Verguier and Ascension Valley
(Tour Map 4)
11kms, 6.8miles, 2.75hours

Park at Le Verguier *Mairie*. Take the Hargicourt road at the eastern end of the main street. This falls away sharply and then climbs to meet the D57 at the site of Priel Crater. Turn left towards Hargicourt and then immediately take a gravel track on the east side of the road. After 350m turn right towards the farm. Follow the grass path to the left of the farm boundary fence and drop down to the lane below. Turn left.

400m on, a track comes in from the right. Straight on goes down to

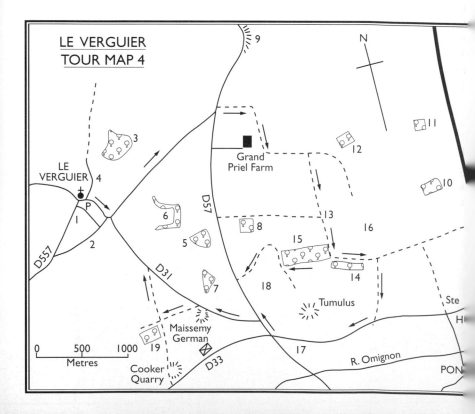

The eastern approaches of Le Verguier. The trees on the left are part of Mill Spinney. British trenches, which included the defended posts known as Orchard, Bob and Bobtail, ran along the crest in front of the village. The more substantial positions of Fort Bell and Fort Greathead were on the reverse slope respectively to the right and left of the village.

Ascension Valley. This is a pleasant secluded walk but, as there is no real way out of the valley bottom, you must eventually retrace your steps. Take the track to the right and walk along Ascension Spur to the trees which mark the site of Ascension Farm **(13)**. Continue along the spur and after another 1000m the track comes to the eastern face of Red Wood **(15)**. This high point provides good views over the valley, Big and Little Bill and the 4th Australian Division memorial. If the crops are growing, turn right and walk down the southern face of Red

LE VERGUIER
TOUR MAP 4

N

9

LE VERGUIER 4

3

Grand
Priel Farm

11

12

10

P

1

6

D57

8

13

16

2

5

15

D31

7

14

18

Tumulus

Ste

H

500   1000
Metres

19

Maissemy
German

Cooker
Quarry

D33

17

R. Omignon

PON

Taken from the lane which leads from Ste Hélène to Victoria Crossroads, the canopy of trees in the far distance is Little Bill. The tops of the trees beneath it belong to Big Bill and the rather sparse wood on the left is Ascension Wood. On 18 September, Australians of the 14th Battalion fought their way across the valley and through the three woods.

Wood. Go right at the bottom and follow the track round to the left. It joins the D57 a little north of the road up to Le Verguier.

If the fields are passable, walk from Red Wood down the slope to Somerville Wood (**14**). On the opposite slope a small road comes in from the right. (This road curls around to cross the motorway via Victoria Crossroads, west of the Australian 4th Division memorial). Take the track on the right and drop down its gentle slope. After 1500m join the D33 west of St Hélène. Turn right along the road. The distinctive mound of the Tumulus is passed after 800m. Mustard Quarry, a former company HQ position, was in the field on the south side of the road (**17**). Turn north onto the D57 at the crossroads. Watling Street joined this road a few metres north of the junction. Its original line can be discerned easily on the slope to the east of the road. Hodson's Post (**18**) was on the slope beneath Red Wood. Take the left fork onto the D31 and walk up towards Le Verguier. Faggot Wood is on your right. Immediately after the quarry on the left, take the track which goes along to Dean Copse (**19**). At the copse, turn right and head back towards the D31. Turn left at the road and continue to Le Verguier.

Shorn of its summer foliage and undergrowth, the ancient tumulus can be seen as a still significant mound. Its surface bears testimony to the attention it received from the artillery of both sides during the war.

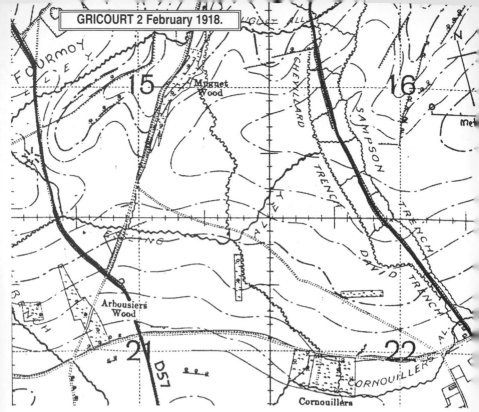

GRICOURT 2 February 1918.

The effects of shell fire on the N29 between Amiens and St Quentin.
Despite its battered state, the road became one of the principal arteries
of the British advance in March and April 1917.

Chapter Five

FRESNOY AND GRICOURT

Fresnoy-le-Petit is a small village on top of a fairly significant rise to the south of the Omignon. To the north the land falls away sharply to Cornouillers Valley, before again rising to climb Hill 120. It then descends quickly to what in 1917 was the remains of Berthaucourt. One mile down the road from Fresnoy to the west is Gricourt. This village, rather larger than its near neighbour, lies in a depression and is separated from Fresnoy by Marronniers Wood. Once the western end of Cornouillers Valley is crossed, the land rises quickly to a narrow plateau before falling away just as sharply to Pontruet. Running roughly parallel to the west of the main Gricourt–Pontruet road is an ancient sunken lane. Passing about 400m to the east of Gricourt, this lane connected Pontruet with the Bellenglise-St Quentin road. On the high ground to the south of Gricourt, and protecting the village from any encroachment from that direction, are two large and one small copses.

In April 1917 two British divisions approached the two villages - the 61st from the south-west and west, and the 32nd from the south. Citing as evidence the division's advance through Fayet to Gricourt, the *Official History* praises the 32nd for having adapted to what it calls the 'new style of semi-open warfare'.[1] The capture of the two large copses, later named Dee and Dum, by the 11/Border opened the way for an attack on Gricourt. The 35th Division moved into the sector, sending the 17/LF through into the village. There was only sporadic resistance from the *451st Infantry Regiment,* and within a few hours the Fusiliers had cleared the ruins.

Like most British troops east of Péronne, members of the 61st Division had spent much of March road-making. The deliberate destruction and mining of roads by the enemy was designed to slow and hamper the British pursuit. The weather was awful and despite the issue of a new groundsheet which doubled as a cape, the troops of 182 and 183 Brigades were extremely wet when they attacked Fresnoy on the night of 7-8 April. The 2/8 Worcester, which had earlier established posts in Cartenoy Wood, moved off to cooperate with the 2/6 Warwick's advance across Cornouillers Valley and up Hill 120. The Worcesters gained the crest but the 2/4 Gloucester's advance towards Fresnoy failed. Hill 120 had obviously been evacuated in a hurry. The new arrivals discovered burning candles and unfinished rations in empty dugouts. Later that day, in the face of strong opposition, the 2/7 Warwick succeeded in taking Fresnoy. As brigades of the 35th Division came into the area, those of the 61st withdrew towards Vermand for a rest.

The 35th Division attacked north and east from Gricourt and Fresnoy. Advancing up the Omignon Valley, the North Midlanders of the 59th Division aimed to meet the 35th in Berthaucourt or Pontruet. The 18/LF took a position called Three Savages on the old sunken lane east of Gricourt. Some reports suggest that there was a substantial farm on the site, while others, including several contemporary maps, indicate that there were no physical remains. Whatever the exact state or nature of the position, it would in the coming days become the scene of several ferocious attacks by both sides. As it was overlooked by German positions west of the Bellenglise–St Quentin road, the Fusiliers withdrew. When it was decided to reoccupy the site, subsequent attacks by the 15/SF and the 19/DLI were met with violent counter-attacks by the enemy. The site became something of a point of honour. For the British it meant they occupied a post – albeit at a disadvantage – close to the Hindenburg outpost line; to the Germans it

British troops, possibly of the 59th Division, fraternize with village children in Bouvincourt, east of Péronne, in March 1917.

was an advanced post just that little too close to their wire.

The more northerly advance on 15 April by 104 Brigade had taken some trenches on the Pontruet Ridge. The following day the 23/Manchester entered the deserted village of Pontruet. At the same time, the 17/West Yorks of 106 Brigade, rushed through and seized the crossroads – or the crater which now replaced what once had been the crossroads – west of Ste Hélêne. The 18/LF, advancing to the west of the Prince of Wales's Own, established posts guarding the river crossings north of Berthaucourt. After some delay, contact was finally made with the 2/4 Berkshire of 184 Brigade. This was as far as the British were going to get. Although they conducted many raids, for example one by the 16/Cheshire on Sycamores Wood on 29 April, the Germans were now at their intended positions. Any further British advance would have to take them through the outpost line and onto the Hindenburg Line itself. Now was not the time to attempt such a breakthrough. More important battles were being fought east of Arras, and a summer campaign near Ypres was already in preparation.

Elements of the Cavalry Corps and a French division relieved the 35th and 61st Divisions in May 1917. The area south of the Omignon remained garrisoned by French troops until January 1918, when once again the 61st Division returned to the sector. International Post, so named because it was where the French and British lines joined, lay on the Omignon north of Berthaucourt. During a very wet and stormy night in January 1918 the post was raided by the Germans and three men of the 2/4 Berks and the 11/Hussars were carried off to the German lines. Pontruet village was also occasionally penetrated by enemy patrols, but they, like the British, thought the ruins to be largely untenable.

The 61st Division spent most of January and February realigning the former French defences and digging Essling redoubt on Hill 120. On 21 March 1/North Staffs of 72 Brigade garrisoned Essling, which **March 1918** was far from complete, and the Forward Zone to the east and north-east. Enemy assault troops poured over Sampson Trench, through C Company's HQ at Muguet Wood and on to Essling redoubt. A Company under the command of Lieutenant Tattersall (who later died in German hands), was soon captured. Across the divisional boundary to their right, the 5/Gordon Highlanders manned Fresnoy redoubt. This stronghold was constructed around the crossroads in the centre of the village, with Battalion HQ and the counter-attack company just to the west. The right and left front companies held Gricourt and the Forward Zone either side of the village; they were soon washed away in the

Lieutenant Ker.

Second Lieutenant John Buchan.

German tide. A runner reported to Battalion HQ at 10.00am with news that the enemy was advancing up Cornouillers Valley. At about the same time, machine-gun fire began falling on the redoubt from the left and right rear. Germans had penetrated to the north and south of the redoubt, but its garrison held on until about 1.00pm. When continued resistance was realised to be pointless, about 30 men escaped to the rear. With one wounded man and a sergeant, Lieutenant Ker of the Gordons and 61st MGC kept the Germans at bay for over three hours, first with a Vickers and then with their revolvers. Ker was later awarded the VC for his action.

Another VC was won by Second Lieutenant John Buchan of the 1/8 Argyll & Sutherland Highlanders. This battalion manned the Battle Zone behind the Gordons. Buchan's position on high ground west of Cartenoy Wood was almost surrounded, yet although gravely wounded, Buchan refused to surrender. Most of the Argylls withdrew to Spooner redoubt above Villecholles, where they fought a resolute delaying action on 22 March. The reserve battalion of 183 Brigade, the 1/9 Royal Scots, was ordered up from Beauvois to relieve the Argylls in the Battle Zone on 22 March. However, the order was almost immediately cancelled and the battalion withdrew to Villévèque.

183 Brigade had put up a strong and sustained resistance. Troops in the Battle Zone had done what was expected of them but, as units to the north withdrew, the position of the Argylls and Royal Scots became untenable. A later report criticised the attitude of troops who, it argued, had become 'over sensitive of their flanks'.[2] Brigadier-General Spooner believed that too many senior officers were obsessed with the belief that, no matter what the circumstances, every yard should be held. Far too many men, he wrote, were pushed into the forward positions with little regard to the concept of defence in depth. Any attempt to withdraw men from front to rear positions in order to gain depth was taken by troops in the rear and on the flanks as a signal for general retirement. Too many officers had prematurely discounted the value of the rifle, while machine-gun crews were too concerned about losing their guns; they did not push forward far enough and retired too early. That might have been an accurate assessment of several units on 21 March, but it was not a fair reflection of the stand made by Spooner's own brigade. Although only one of the Gordon's officers was actually killed that day, when the remaining 60 members of the

battalion were ordered to counter-attack near Berthencourt on 24 March, they did so under the command of the MO. He was the only officer to survive the first day's battle.

When in September 1918 British forces were again approaching the Hindenburg Line, the 1st, 6th and elements of the 46th Divisions were charged with the responsibility of retaking the area lost by the 24th and 61st Divisions. Having cleared the high ground south of Maissemy on 15 September, the 1/SWB relieved the 1/KSLI and 1/Buffs of 16 Brigade in the line opposite Fresnoy. Meanwhile, the 2/KRRC had taken Berthaucourt and was warned that on 24 September it would go for Cornouillers Valley while the 2/Sussex and 1/Northants went for Essling redoubt and the slope running down to Pontruet. The 5/Leicester of 138 Brigade would attempt to take the village itself.

September 1918

2 Brigade began well. It met stiff opposition but the Sussex moved over the site of Essling and into the remains of Sampson Trench. The Rifles skirmished along Cornouillers Valley, taking Arbousiers and Cornouillers Woods. However, the Leicesters were having a very tough time to their left in Pontruet. Two companies tried to outflank the village from the north while two made a frontal attack. After very heavy fighting they captured the civilian cemetery and a blockhouse nearby. Enemy resistance stiffened still further and a bombing party forced the Leicesters from Forgan's Trench. Lieutenant J.Barrett led his platoon against the trench, and although

Lieutenant John Barrett.

wounded three times, knocked out two machine guns. Despite his bravery, which was later recognised by the award of a VC, the Leicesters were getting nowhere. At 1.40am on 25 September they were forced to withdraw from Pontruet.

Their lack of progress affected the left flank of 2 Brigade. The 1/Northants had to give ground on the slopes above Pontruet which, in turn exposed the left of the Sussex. When about 400 Germans launched a counter-attack against the Sussex, Captain Roberts ordered his company to charge with fixed bayonets. Although outnumbering the Sussex by five to one, the Germans were routed. Nevertheless, the battalion had suffered severely. Following the action of 18 September one company had already been reduced to three platoons and now, with another four subalterns dead, four wounded and two missing, three companies were reorganised as a composite unit. The fourth was considered strong enough to man the outpost line.

The 2/KRRC had suffered too, but not as severely. The Rifles were ordered to take over a stretch of Sampson Trench occupied by the

Sussex. HQ was sited in Muguet Wood where, for two days, it was subjected to intense shelling. It was essential that the brigade retain its grip on Sampson in order to prevent German observation over the preparations going on in the dead ground for the next attack. Companies of the divisional RE and Pioneers came up during the night of 24-25 to assist the Rifles with consolidation.

While 2 Brigade was passing to the north of Fresnoy and Gricourt, 3 and 16 Brigades attacked the village from the south. The 2/York & Lancs had managed to get into Fresnoy six days earlier, but its stay had been cut short by a ferocious counter- attack. In the early hours of 24 September, 1/Gloucester on the left and 2/Welch on the right took over the positions held by the 1/SWB since 21 September. The Welch advanced quite successfully down the slope towards the Gricourt-Fresnoy road, with 16 Brigade and Dee Copse on their right. The Gloucesters took Fresnoy cemetery and the nearby strongpoint, capturing four officers and 160 men, five trench mortars and several machine guns in the process. The captives included a very indignant battalion CO who loudly voiced criticism of his divisional command for not warning him of the assault. Strong opposition came from the garrison of the stepped trench falling away to Cornouillers Wood, but by 5.30pm the Gloucesters had linked up with 16 Brigade in Gricourt. However, one determined centre of resistance remained to be cleared within Fresnoy. This strongpoint was sited in the village's north-west corner, not far from the former HQ of the 5/Gordon Highlanders. The Gloucesters tried to pinch it out from the west and south. Any of the garrison who attempted to surrender were shot by their own officers. British artillery was again brought down on the position and a plan drawn up to storm it from three sides at 10.30pm. Shortly before Zero, 14 Germans managed to evade their officers and surrendered. They indicated the site of the strongpoint's HQ and a trench mortar bombardment was hastily arranged to deal with it. That did the trick, for when the infantry followed behind, five officers and 124 other ranks emerged from their dugouts and surrendered. 16 Brigade to the east had cleared Gricourt and pushed its outpost line as far as the Three Savages.

1st and 6th Divisions were now in occupation of roughly the same positions defended by the 61st on 21 March. The two divisions knew that the next stage of the advance would of necessity be against the Hindenburg Line. In the initial stages of the assault their roles were to be largely passive. This was probably just as well for they were both very under-strength. Both divisions needed a respite to absorb and train new drafts. Having been relieved by a French division, the 6th Division was to be allowed such a period. The 1st was not so fortunate. It barely had time to draw breath before it was called upon to support the crossing of the St Quentin Canal by the 46th and 32nd Divisions.

Notes

1. *Official History 1917*, p.528
2. Report by Brigadier-General A.Spooner, 6 April 1918, appended to War Diary of 5/Gordon Highlanders. WO.95.3061

Fresnoy and Gricourt today

The hill top village of Fresnoy is little more than a small gathering of houses clustered around a central crossroads. Grain silos to the west stand out as rather ugly landmarks and a large modern farm complex serves a similar function to the south. The silos are on the track which passes Cartenoy Wood and Otter Copse. The site of the German stronghold which delayed the advance of the 1/Gloucester in September 1918 is probably the area of scrub and bush between the house with a satellite dish and the large farm. **(1)** The only significant building in the village itself is the chateau just north and west of the crossroads. Marronniers Wood offers a pleasant touch of summer green but is private property at the village end. It can be entered east of the communal cemetery **(2)**, at the crucifix. The cemetery has a large family plot, one of whose members was a former representative of the Conseil-General of the Department of the Aisne. There is a group of 19 French soldiers of the 47th Division. These men possibly succumbed to wounds or were brought in from another area as by the time they died the battles had moved well to the east.

Gricourt is a larger village, with its approaches and centre often augmented by communal flower displays. It has a well maintained Mairie and a pleasant aspect. Pontruet too shows signs of recent incomers - comfortable new housing with tended gardens lies on its

With Cartenoy Wood on the left, Arbousiers Wood can be seen on the opposite slope of Cornouillers Valley. The water tower marks the site of Essling redoubt. Today, instead of the several communication trenches which wound along and across the valley, deer are often seen gambolling among the crops.

eastern side. The blockhouse where Lieutenant Barrett won his VC is no more, the site now being occupied by a dingy dwelling. **(3)** Nearby, the civilian cemetery has been replaced by a grassed area overlooked by a crucifix. The D73 runs west to what was in 1918 the ruins of Berthaucourt. Although this village was larger than Pontru, it was Pontru which absorbed its bigger neighbour. There remains only a Rue de Berthaucourt to remind visitors of its former separate existence. The Omignon flows lethargically to its north, marking what had in 1917 been the boundary between French and British units. International Post lay in the valley between the two villages. **(4)**

Berthaucourt Communal Cemetery is sited on the D73 to Maissemy.

Tour of Fresnoy and Gricourt
(Tour Map 5)
8.4kms, 5.25miles. 1.75hours

Park at Gricourt *Mairie*. A minor road at the village crossroads heads across the motorway and continues on to the N44. The Three Savages is now under the motorway but there is a pleasant walk up an old road which led past the site and connected Pontruet with the Bellenglise-St Quentin road. This can be reached by walking past the football stadium. However, an easier route is to head north from Gricourt on the D732. As the road climbs out of the village, Cornouillers Wood is to the west. **(5)** The road runs roughly between Sampson and Chevillard Trenches. The importance to the British of the highest point on the ridge can be easily appreciated. As the road drops towards Pontruet, Muguet Wood is on the left. **(6)**

Walk over the first crossroads and turn left at the village war memorial. The ancient road from the Three Savages reaches the village behind the memorial and here is known as the *Chausée d'Arras*. Go through the housing, past the crucifix and the former cemetery, turn right immediately after and follow the track over the Omignon. **(3)** This

Often used as a company or battalion HQ, Muguet Wood sits comfortably in a valley behind the extensive front line system centred along Sampson and Brient Trenches. The buildings of Bellenglise can be seen in the dip beyond the wood. The photo looks north-east from Essling redoubt.

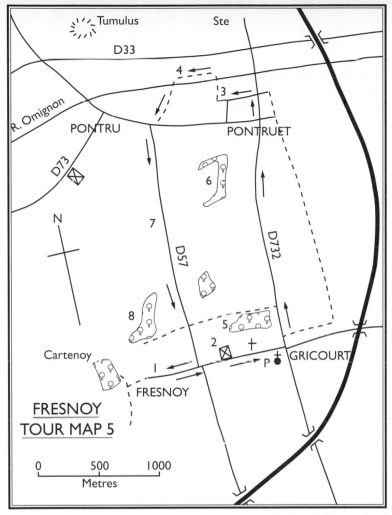

**FRESNOY
TOUR MAP 5**

0   500   1000

Metres

was the area where Lieutenant Barrett won his VC. Continue north of the river for 300m, turn left to recross it and then on into Berthaucourt. International Post was in the flat land to your right. **(4)**

In the village turn left towards Fresnoy (D57). Climb up to the water tower (Essling redoubt). **(7)** Fourmoy Alley (a communication trench) crossed the road 400m north of the tower. As the road falls away to Cornouillers Valley, Arbousiers Wood is on the right. **(8)** Climb up to Fresnoy and turn right at the crossroads to visit the site of the German stronghold. **(1)** Return to the crossroads and go straight over. This is the road to Gricourt. Fresnoy civilian cemetery is on the left. **(2)** Follow the edge of Marronniers Wood and enter by the crucifix. There are some vestiges of trenches on the slopes. Gricourt *Mairie* is 300m on down the road.

British troops, possibly of the 61st Division, await the order to advance in improvised trenches west of St Quentin, April 1917.

Chapter Six

FAYET AND HOLNON

Lying only a few miles west of St Quentin, the villages of Fayet, Holnon and Selency had been victims of German aggression in January 1871. General Faidherbe's attack on the German-held town of St Quentin elicited a strong and decisive riposte from General von Goeben's First Army. Faidherbe's force, low in morale and weary from marches in drenching rain, was fatally divided on opposite sides of the Somme. Goeben's thrust up the west bank of the river caught the poorly led troops of XXIII Corps in the fields west of St Quentin. Although its defeat was total, inhabitants of the villages through which the bedraggled army had first advanced and then withdrawn, later erected several memorials to their compatriots who had fallen within their fields and streets.

Another German First Army also marched through the area in August 1914. General Maunoury's French Sixth Army engaged its outer wing, while to the east of St Quentin, General Lanrezac's forces fought delaying actions between the town and Guise. Elements of British II Corps passed along its streets following their action at Le Cateau. The celebrated intervention of Tom Bridges and his batman persuaded the weary men of two battalions to get back on their feet and away. The town fell, and was to remain in German hands until 1 October 1918.

To ensure the safety of the railhead and to take advantage of the billeting facilities offered by St Quentin, the Germans sited the Hindenburg Line to the west of the built up area. This caused a

German troops massing in St Quentin preparatory to their offensive of March 1918. The railway junction was a pivotal point of the German advance.

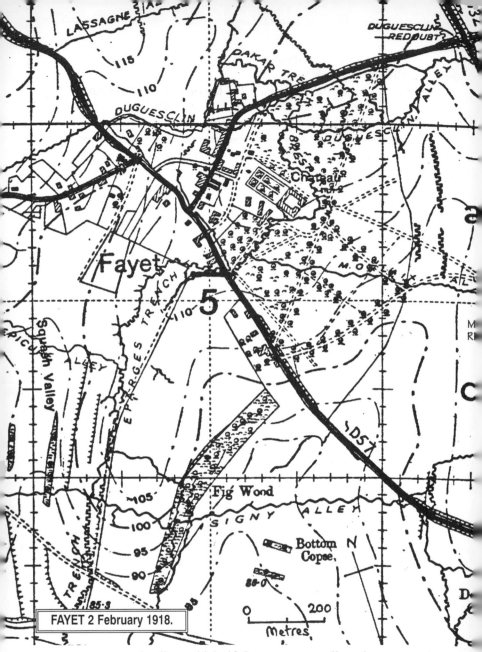

LASSAGNE

DUGUESCLIN
REDOUBT

DAKAR TRE

DUGUESCLIN

BREST

Château

DUGUESCLIN

N. ALLEY

115

110

Fayet

TRENCH

EPARGES TRENCH

5

110

MOST

ALL

Squash Valley

ALLEY

DST

C

M
R

105

100

95

90

85·3

86

TRENCH

Fig Wood

SIGNY   ALLEY

Bottom
Copse.

88·0

N

D

0   200
Metres

FAYET 2 February 1918.

pronounced salient which, if the enemy was allowed to approach too
close, would give him observation down the valleys into the town. The
German intention was therefore to retain their grip on Holnon,
Francilly-Selency and Fayet as outpost positions. Possession of these

villages and the land around them would deny Allied observation over the main Hindenburg Line.

The capture of the villages by the 32nd Division in April 1917 put paid to the German scheme. The 2/KOYLI and 16/HLI took Fayet, while the 1/Dorset pushed on to Cepy Farm on the high ground beyond. This was the third time since the war began that Fayet had seen armies in action. In August, and again in September 1914, French and German armies had clashed; now it was the turn of the BEF to occupy its broken buildings. The operation was later described as being a

> *'fine example of good organisation, judicious delegation of authority and quick movement, allied with determination'.*[1]

Built within a depression, Fayet would not be easy to defend; ground to the north and east would first have to be secured before the village could be considered tenable. The key to this were the twin copses to the north, subsequently taken by the Lonsdales, and the area around Cepy Farm. The further the British could establish themselves towards the St Quentin-Bellenglise road, the more secure would be Fayet.

As they left, men of the 32nd Division related tales to the incoming 61st of poor morale among troops of the *451st Infantry Regiment*. These soldiers had, according to the 32nd, 'failed signally to exhibit any fighting qualities'.[2] In an effort to capitalise upon this intelligence, on 28 April the 2/4 Ox & Bucks raided German trenches near Squaw Copse and Indian Wood. Instead of encountering demoralised troops of the *234th Division*, the Ox & Bucks came up against very serious opposition from the *3rd Jaeger*. Having suffered nearly 60 casualties, the somewhat surprised raiders withdrew.

The 2/4 Berkshire also experienced strong opposition when it made several attempts against Cepy Farm. Twenty-four hours after the raid by the Ox & Bucks, patrols discovered the farm to be empty at night but occupied during the day. On 30 April the battalion attacked the buildings with the intention of denying their use to the Germans. The enemy fled and, after posting a garrison, most of the Berkshires withdrew. The Germans then returned and turfed out the Berkshires. This process was repeated several times until the division was withdrawn and replaced by French III Corps.

French forces developed the area's defences, naming many of them after national heroes and French towns. Although it appeared impressively extensive on maps, the system was not to the liking of 61st Division when it returned in January 1918 to relieve the 74th Regiment. The division came down from the Villers-Plouich sector after having endured an unpleasant tour on the slopes about La

British troops complained of the poor state of the former French trenches when they took over the St Quentin sector from their ally. Here, the leading officer at least has the advantage of trench waders. <small>TAYLOR LIBRARY</small>

Vacquerie. French laches over the design of their defences was criticised in a scathing report written by a member of 182 Brigade.[3] The author concluded that the existing system was 'extensive but not...of much use as defensive works'. None of the trenches were revetted, few had usable fire-steps and even fewer were fitted with duckboards. The outpost line was in an exceptionally poor state. Each post had a field of fire of only about 40m with the wire far too close to the parapet. Communications between them and by the communication trenches to the rear were also considered to be very bad. The redoubt line was only partially constructed, although its wire was generally adequate. Owing to the almost complete absence of shell holes it was assumed a tacit 'live and let live' system had operated between the French and Germans. One of the few aspects the report did not criticise was the dugout accommodation. This was thought to be spacious and well constructed, which was just as well because the increasing number of very young soldiers then being drafted to the brigade found tours in these trenches 'very trying'. Neither did the report find fault with the French names. One or two Englishmen with a knowledge of Anglo-French history might have found it somewhat strange to occupy a trench named in honour of Bernard du Guesclin.

Enghien redoubt was constructed on the west side of a small road between Fayet and Selency. It was well sited, enjoying good observation across Squash Valley and the approaches to St Quentin. In the early stages of the German attack on 21 March, forward companies of the 2/4 Ox & Bucks in and around Dee and Dum Copses to the north of the redoubt largely disappeared. The redoubt itself quickly came under fire from north and south. D Company and Battalion HQ held out in the redoubt and the quarry immediately to its south until about 4.00pm when German trench mortars and field artillery were brought up to pound the site. The garrison tried to fight its way out and join with other stragglers from the forward companies who had attached themselves to the 2/5 Gloucester in the Battle Zone. One report suggests that perhaps only one officer and two men escaped.[4] In total, officer casualties among the Ox & Bucks that day were given as 14 missing, four missing and believed killed and one wounded and missing. Other rank figures were five killed, 22 wounded and 425 missing.

On 22 March the 2/5 Gloucester was positioned on high ground just about where the minor road from Maissemy joined the main Vermand–Holnon road. Offering magnificent targets to the Gloucesters in the Battle Zone, the Germans attacked in fine sunshine. They first had to climb up the slope from Otter Copse, before then crossing 1000m of open ground. The Gloucesters checked several attacks but, with the enemy penetration down the Omignon Valley to their left, the battalion withdrew across the main road, through Sword Wood and on towards Attilly.

The right brigade of the 61st Division was 182. Its forward battalion, with a hugely extended front of nearly two miles, was the 2/8 Worcester. Two forward companies manned a series of posts between Roses Wood and Fayet. These positions were linked by shallow trenches and laid out to give mutually supporting covering fire. The counter-attack company was divided between Squash Valley and Fayet, with the fourth, along with Battalion HQ, in Ellis redoubt. This redoubt was incomplete but well sited. It consisted of a ring of connected posts spreading down the southern slope of the Holnon–St Quentin road about 400m east of Selency. Besides the Lewis guns and rifles of B Company, it also contained two trench mortars and probably two Vickers.

As March wore on, the divisional staff grew increasingly suspicious of German intent. The enemy was so unnaturally quiet in the days leading up to the assault that Corps ordered a large-scale gas bombardment against St Quentin during the night of 19-20 March. Its effect on the Germans was unknown but it did cause 19 Worcesters to be sent back for treatment. This was followed by a raid of two companies of the 2/6 Warwick. The raiders left theWorcesters' forward posts in Fayet and managed to capture 12 prisoners from a newly arrived division. The Warwicks lost Second Lieutenant Houghton but, from the number of Germans seen and heard in the front trenches, and from intelligence learned through interrogating the captives, it was confirmed that a major attack was imminent.

The entire concept of forward posts offering mutual support was nullified by the morning mist of 21 March. Fayet fell almost immediately, a few survivors of B Company escaping back to Ellis. Miraculously a telephone cable between an OP in Fig Wood and Ellis remained intact throughout the bombardment. The signaller just had time to report that the enemy was upon them before the line went dead. Two platoons of D Company in Squash Valley were surrounded before they knew what was happening, although some did manage to fight their way through to the redoubt. By 11.30am the mist was gone. Defenders in Ellis saw hordes of Germans sweeping past on the high ground to the north and along the valley to their south. Infantry assaults on the redoubt were supported by further bombardments. Wounded from the redoubt were evacuated during a lull in the fighting in the early afternoon. Most of them appear to have been killed on the way out, but those who did run the gauntlet and survived, arrived at Holnon only to discover it to be in German hands. By late afternoon Ellis was isolated. Enghien and Manchester Hill fell at about 4.00pm, so the German tide flowed freely and largely untroubled either side of Ellis. The redoubt came under concentrated crossfire and was finally rushed at about 5.30pm. Fourteen of its garrison later reported at the battalion's transport lines.

With 183 Brigade to the north, all three of the 61st Division's brigades maintained their hold on the Battle Zone throughout the first two days of the battle. Lieutenant-General Ivor Maxse, GOC XVIII Corps, acknowledged their stand in a congratulatory message of early April.[5] He described how the three 'heroic' front line battalions were attacked by at least three divisions and that despite being ordered to fight their way out at 4.00pm on 21 March,

'very few returned...They simply fought it out on the spot and

their heroism will live forever in the annals of their regiments'.
It remains unclear whether the survivors of all three battalions ever did receive the corps order allowing withdrawal. Nevertheless, at the cost of very heavy losses, the Battle Zone and its defenders had done what was expected of them.

In the same way as the 61st Division made it difficult for the Germans in March, the new defenders of Enghien, Ellis and the neighbouring villages were equally determined to exact a heavy cost of the September attackers. On the 18th, Holnon was drenched with gas. 18 Brigade passed either side of it but the 2/DLI, whose objective was to the south of the village, was particularly hard hit by fire coming from its right. An attempt on Manchester Hill and Round Hill by the French 34th Division had failed, thus exposing the Durhams to

withering enfilade fire. A draft arrived during the day and the battalion was again hurled against the trenches immediately to the south of Ellis. At the end of the day, the Durhams' casualty list was longer than the muster roll of those who had taken part in the morning's attack.

A copse now grows on the site of Enghien redoubt. There were remains of cottages on the mound when the French began to fortify the position in 1917, but the ruins there today are of post-war vintage.

On the left, 71 Brigade attacked the former Enghien redoubt. Since March the Germans had expended considerable effort in realigning the British trenches and strengthening the wire. The position, which incorporated the quarry to its south, could be reinforced safely from the rear, had superb fields of fire to the north, south and west and had all the sunken lanes leading towards it filled with concertina wire. The British had renamed the position the Quadrilateral. The 2/SF and 9/Norfolk secured and then lost a toe-hold on its western edge, and another attempt by the 1/Leicester later in the day was also repulsed. 71 Brigade had fallen foul of poor communications, impenetrable wire and the fire of an untold number of machine guns. The Norfolks and Leicesters sought what shelter they could find in the valleys near Badger and Kirchner Copses, while the Foresters squirmed into any folds in the ground in front of the redoubt. Divisional staff realised that the position could only be taken after a prolonged and methodical period of preparation. There was a pause for five days which allowed the French to come up on the right and for the artillery to drop in one day 1000 shells onto the Quadrilateral. On 24 September, the 6th Division tried again. Assisted by four tanks, 16 Brigade went for the trenches running towards the objective from the north, while 18 Brigade, with another four tanks, assaulted the redoubt from the west and north-west. One tank turned turtle after hitting a mine at the commencement of the assault, but the remaining three helped the 11/Essex to get a slight hold on the western edge and the 1/West Yorks to enter Douai Trench to its north. However, progress remained slow and tortuous. It took a night attack to finally secure the position and another two days of bombing to clear the trenches to its east. Surrendering German officers insisted they had believed their position to be impregnable.

Enghien and Ellis redoubts had again fallen, and once again had done so at tremendous cost. The 6th Division was too exhausted to continue, so French XV Corps pushed across Squash Valley and up to Fayet. It was to take another three days for the corps to break the Hindenburg Line, liberate St Quentin and join hands with the British 1st Division east of the canal.

Notes

1. *Official History 1917*, p.528
2. War Diary of 2/4 Ox and Bucks, 28 April 1917. WO.95.3067
3. Report in War Diary of 2/7 Warwick, 11 January 1918. WO.95.3056
4. M.Middlebrook, *The Kaiser's Battle*, p.263
5. Report by Lieutenant-General I.Maxe, 10 April 1918, appended to War Diary of 2/6 Warwick. WO.95.3056

Fayet and Holnon today

One of the most attractive and best maintained villages in the district, Fayet's war memorial merits a visit in its own right. **(1)** Sited near the *Mairie*, it has two plaques. One commemorates the battles in and around its confines on 28 August and 16 September 1914, the period of trench warfare between March 1917 and March 1918 and the liberation of the ruins on 30 September by the French 46th and 47th Divisions. Its partner records the transportation of able-bodied males by the Germans in February 1917 to Marpent near Maubeuge, and of the women, children and elderly to Noyon a few days later. The Germans next proceeded to destroy the village, having already felled the woods and cleared the scrub between April 1916 and May 1917. A modern and exclusive housing estate fills the southern part of the village.

The beautifully maintained war memorial at Fayet.

Cepy Farm **(2)** still sits on the eastern side of the D732. It is a large enclosure but looks to have suffered from its proximity to a built-up area. Fig Wood **(3)** to the south-west of Fayet contains the remains of British trenches and the telephone post where a soldier of the 2/8 Worcester reported the commencement of the German attack on 21 March.

The copse which now stands on Enghien redoubt is easily visited. **(4)** The ruined buildings on its northern face have nothing to do with the wartime occupancy and the quarry to its south is largely filled and enclosed within the grounds of a modern house. Standing on the western face of the redoubt, the superb fields of fire enjoyed by the Germans who garrisoned the Quadrilateral in September 1918 can be well appreciated.

Lying beneath a garden centre on the southern side of the N29 almost opposite the junction with the C3, Ellis redoubt **(5)** is more difficult to see. The site is best observed from the water tower **(6)** on an unmade road running from Selency to St Quentin. There are three memorials by the church at Selency. **(7)** One is to the French forces

A memorial at Francilly-Selency to the French troops who died in the battle of January 1871. This is a fairly recent memorial and might have been erected to replace the one originally sited near Roses Wood.

who fought here in 1871, the second is the village war memorial and the third commemorates two battalions of the Manchester Regiment - the regular 2nd Battalion, which as part of the 33rd Division liberated the area in April 1917, and the 16th Battalion, which held Manchester Hill on 21 March. There was another monument to the 1871 fighting built on a track east of the motorway. **(8)** It lay near what was Roses Wood on the spur north of the road running past the water tower. The site is now perpetually overgrown, awkward, painful to bare arms and legs and unconvincing once through the defences. The position was later built over and its more recent buildings fester to rubble among the nettles.

Holnon is another delightful village. It has an interesting war memorial and an attractive, if functional square. Near a small roundabout on its western edge is another memorial to the fighting of January 1871. **(9)** The road to the west drives on into Holnon Wood. The wood now contains picnic benches and is a favourite route for weekend mountain bikers. If you value your suspension, do not attempt to drive into the wood. Between April 1917 and March 1918 the wood was used extensively by British troops and guns. Chapelle British Cemetery **(10)** is 50m south of the N29. An unmade sunken lane heading north from the N29 at a small crossroads 300m west of the cemetery reveals evidence of several British dugouts mined into its eastern bank. **(11)**

Holnon's war memorial in the Marraine de Guerre d'Holnon. As well as the usual list of names from the two world wars, the memorial also commemorates a local man killed during the French occupation of Indochina in 1883.

Tour of Fayet and Holnon

(Tour Map 6)

17kms, 10.6miles. 3.75 hours

Park at Fayet *Mairie*. Take the small road behind the war memorial which goes up to the N44. Du Guesclin redoubt was at the crossroads of the present road and the D732 from Gricourt. Indian and Tomahawk Woods can be seen to the north-east. Turn right onto the D732 towards St Quentin. This road runs immediately behind what was the British outpost line in March 1918. 1200m on is Cepy Farm. **(2)** Turn back and take the *Rue de Lille*, a residential road running through a new housing estate. After 800m the road comes to a T-junction at traffic lights. Turn right onto Rue de Fayet (D57).

As you approach Fayet, take the left fork onto *Rue Pierre Currie* and left again onto *Rue l'Epinette*. This road becomes a track, with an offshoot going off left to Fig Wood. **(3)** This spur provides good views

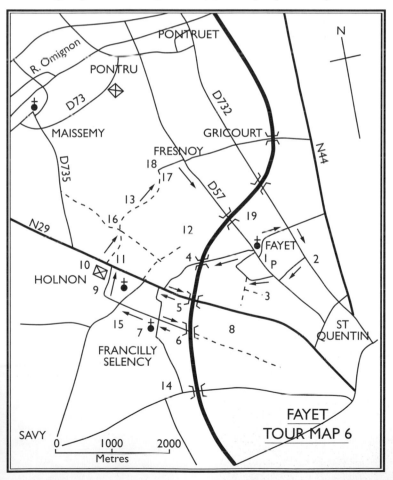

Ellis redoubt lay on the slope facing the camera, roughly between the house and the shed. A long communication trench called Ivry Alley ran along the floor of the valley beneath the redoubt. The N29 is on the crest above the redoubt, south of the wood.

over Squash Valley and the site of Enghien redoubt **(4)** to the west and Roses Wood straight on over the opposite slope beyond the N29.

Walk back to Fayet and take the C3 (*Rue Quentin de la Tour*), to cross the motorway and on to Enghien. Walk to the western face of the copse. Kirchner Copse **(12)** can be seen to the north and Otter Copse **(13)** to the north-west. Continue down the road to the N29. Turn left. The site of Ellis redoubt **(5)** is 400m to the east on the south side of the road. Retrace and take the first road on the left into Selency.

Follow this road until the church. Turn left and walk east to the water tower **(6)** for better views of Ellis redoubt and Manchester Hill **(14)** to the south (radio mast nearby). Ivry Valley communication trench ran along the valley beneath Ellis. Walk back to the church and go straight over the crossroads towards Holnon. Round Hill **(15)** is to the south. Chapelle British Cemetery **(10)** is on the north-west side of the village. Get on to the main road, turn left and then right at a small crossroads 300m after the cemetery. The remains of British dugouts can be seen in the bank of the sunken lane. **(11)** After 900m turn left at the junction and then bear right at the underground reservoir. **(16)** This lane leads past Otter Copse **(13)** and a small quarry **(17)** on the right before curling right in front of Cartenoy Wood. **(18)** Until March 1918, the quarry was regularly used by British battalion HQ staff. Follow the lane past the grain silos and into Fresnoy. Turn right at the crossroads onto the D57. Dee and Dum Copses **(19)** are on the east side of the road as it drops down into Fayet.

Enghien redoubt viewed from the west. The trees on the left mark the site and the white house (centre) includes the quarry of the Quadrilateral within its hedges. The wood beyond lies within the former chateau grounds. The photo is taken with Trout Copse on the right and Badger Copse just off to the left.

Chapter Seven

HARGICOURT AND VILLERET

Elements of the British 3rd Division marched through the twin villages of Hargicourt and Villeret on their way south in August 1914; the cottages and farms which constituted the villages would have aroused little interest among the exhausted British troops. The churches, squares and adjoining farms were like a hundred other villages they had passed through during the Retreat. Apart from the odd prisoner of war and the occasional patrolling aircraft, the next British soldiers to see the two villages were those of the 59th Division in April 1917.

Having first taken Templeux-le-Guérard, the 2/North Midland

An aerial view of Templeux le-Guérard and its quarries. Thick belts of wire protect the approaches from Templeux Wood and continue north-east towards Ronssoy.

Transport, guns and ambulances make their way along Hargicourt Valley, 20 September 1918. The village is in almost total ruin.

Division approached Hargicourt from the west. On 5 April the 1/8 Worcester was ordered to attack a nasty piece of ground known as the Mound lying among the quarries north of that village. Although the 59th claimed it had taken Templeux, the Worcesters reported that they had found only 'one scared corporal and two men'[1] in a listening post north of the village. Despite the lack of accurate intelligence and a deep covering of snow, the Worcesters' attack in support of the 59th's advance on Hargicourt and 145 Brigade's attack on Ronssoy and Bassè Boulogne were remarkably successful. To their south 176 Brigade took its objectives of Villeret and Hargicourt Quarries, although a subsequent attack to the north of the quarries by the 2/5 Lincoln failed. A lengthy period of preparation and rehearsals for 178 Brigade later in the month culminated with the capture of the mined area which later became known to the British as Slag Quarry. During this operation, the 2/6 North Staffs won the rubble of what had once been a farm on the eastern slope of Hargicourt; the position was immediately ascribed the sobriquet of Unnamed Farm.

By the end of April the North Midlanders had achieved a rudimentary consolidation of their newly-won acquisitions. Because they enjoyed observation over most of the new British positions, the Germans were not perturbed by the altered arrangements. They had carefully and deliberately chosen the ground on which they were now to stand. These ensured that if the British did attempt to advance further, it would be at a heavy cost; if they chose to remain static, their movements would always be under close scrutiny. For the time being at least, this strategic British disadvantage did not seem unduly to worry the son of the 2/8 Sherwood Foresters' CO. Captain Oates was reported to have sniped an unsuspecting partridge through the head, collected it from No Man's Land during cover of darkness and presented it to his father for supper.

The 59th was relieved by the Cavalry Corps in late April. The cavalry raided the enemy trenches several times during their sojourn, including a fairly large and determined operation on Cologne Farm on the night of 1-2 July. They also worked hard on the trenches, deciding that at the end of their stay the Hargicourt sector was where 'conditions approximate to trench warfare'.[2] When intelligence was received that the New Army 34th and 35th Divisions were moving in to relieve the cavalry, the Brigadier-General of the Cavalry Corps confided his scepticism of the infantry's worth to his diary. In somewhat conceited vein Brigadier-General Sir Archibald Horne decided:

'Their men are not as good as ours and they find it difficult to do the same amount of patrolling as we do'.[3]

Difficult or not, the two Kitchener divisions were destined to make the area east of the two villages a substantially more active sector than it had been during the cavalry's stay.

A few hundred metres east of Hargicourt were the ruins of two farms: Unnamed, incorporated within the British lines, and Cologne. This second farm, which still had some gable ends standing, was 200m to the south of Unnamed and higher up the slope. No Man's Land lay between the two sites. Elsewhere in the sector the trench lines widened out somewhat to a more conventional distance. The area which a few months later was to be developed into the British Battle Zone lay on the higher ground to the west of the village, but as the enemy held the ridge which ran approximately parallel to the British lines, the depression across which British reinforcements and supplies were carried to the front trenches was overlooked by Germans in Cologne

Australian and American engineers and pioneers labour to open up the Hargicourt-Bellicourt road the day after the latter village was captured.

Farm. Patrols went out frequently from both sides and in mid-July a fairly determined enemy raid attempted to enter Unnamed Farm. A week before the German effort a patrol of the 15/Royal Scots had discovered Cologne Farm to be deserted. It was assumed that during daylight hours the farm was usually either unoccupied or only lightly garrisoned.

The GOC 35th Division decided the enemy had to be driven from the Cologne Ridge. New advance trenches were dug and training over mock-ups of the enemy lines began. The attack was scheduled to commence at 4.30am on 26 August on a front stretching 1000m either side of Unnamed Farm. The trenches to be assaulted were about one mile to the west of the Hindenburg Line itself and, if taken, would allow observation over sections of the line. This objective would be achieved if the Red Line was gained - a penetration of the outpost line of about 1000m.

By the early hours of 26 August 101 Brigade had all four battalions in the line ready to assault and the divisional artillery had been supplemented by 76 machine guns directed to fire a barrage over the heads of the attackers. On the left flank the 11/Suffolk, chewing gum

A lorry toils up the slope from Villeret to Hargicourt, September 1918. Villeret is in ruins and the light railway which ran across the road in the valley bottom is not yet relaid. A discarded tank's crib lies in the field to the right. IWM E3772

in an attempt to lessen the chance of troops coughing and alerting the enemy, formed up between Unnamed Farm and Hussar Post in a sunken lane a little in advance of their own line. When the whistles blew, the battalion climbed up the banking and followed the barrage. After some hard hand-to-hand fighting the Suffolks took Malakoff Farm and the trench behind. The 10/Lincoln on its right attacked from Unnamed Farm and swept through to the sugar factory. Some reached the ruins of Ruby Farm and others pressed on as far as Ruby Wood. They captured a number of dazed Germans belonging to the *1st Battalion, 141st Regiment*. The prisoners claimed they were anticipating an attack but had been completely surprised by the intensity of the barrage. Further to the right, the 16/Royal Scots jumped off from either side of Cologne Farm. Easily gaining Pond Trench, the Scots continued on to Bait Trench, 400m in front of Ruby Wood. The right flank battalion was the 15/Royal Scots. It fought its way through from Slag Quarry to a line of posts 300m beyond Railway Trench. The artillery had not made much of an impact on these defences and, within 45 seconds of reaching them, the Scots were forced back to Railway Trench. During the day enemy counter-attacks were fought off but attempts to get reinforcements over to the Scots were frustrated by a German barrage laid in Villeret Valley and by small arms fire emanating from Farm Trench.

During the night it began to rain. The downpour grew in intensity

during 27 August, flooding what little remained of the almost obliterated trenches. In some places the water was waist deep. Repeated German counter-attacks and an incessant bombardment hampered British attempts at consolidation, relief and the passage of supplies. The weather put paid to a proposed attack by 103 Brigade designed to push the Germans from Villeret Col, south of Railway and Farm Trenches. A combination of continuing bad weather and of the current weak strength of the battalions resulted in a postponement of the attack until 9 September. The 20th, 21st and 23/NF of 102 Brigade went over from Villeret towards Farm Trench and Quarry Wood. After some very bitter fighting, the troublesome sections of Farm Trench were consolidated and a communication trench dug from Martin Post to the new positions.

The main purpose of the operation of 26 August had, according to one history, 'been brilliantly achieved'.[4] However, it had cost 101 Brigade heavily. When the brigade was withdrawn its battalions mustered between 400 and 480 men. The 16/Royal Scots had lost over 150, the 11/Suffolk 170, the 10/Lincoln 223 and the 15/Royal Scots 201. Many of the dead lie in Hargicourt British Cemetery and the communal extension. Reports on the operation detailed what had, by

The railway embankment running across to Slag Quarry, captured in September 1918. Numerous dugouts have been tunnelled in to the spoil tips and other workings. IWM E3789

that stage of the war become a familiar story: most casualties occurred after the positions had been won; two water bottles per man were essential; leading waves should carry more picks and shovels; breech covers were indispensable; all ranks should be informed of their objectives and, to prevent them from becoming useless in the wet, Stokes mortar shells should always be carried in boxes. There were the usual problems of British artillery firing short and of communication difficulties with the support aircraft. Perhaps the strangest conclusion was that reached by the diarist of the 11/Suffolk. He cryptically recorded that infantry should 'not...believe heavy gunners'.[5]

The two principal attacks by the 34th and 35th Divisions had won possession of a few very significant yards of front. Ration parties and reliefs could approach the front lines with less anxiety about being spotted, while observers in the British trenches could learn a little more about the intricacies of the wire fields protecting the main enemy positions. By September, when the 24th Division moved into the sector, the enemy had apparently become 'reconciled to the loss of Cologne Farm'[6] and caused the division little trouble. There was the usual unpleasantness from hostile gunners and several battalions regularly undertook raids across No Man's Land. The 1/Northants intended to investigate the area behind Malakoff Farm twice in November 1917, but on both occasions the mud and wire prevented the raiders from penetrating further than an enemy sap. On the night of 19-

20 November, when divisions to the north were about to unleash the Cambrai offensive, the 2/Leinster and the 9/East Surrey attempted to raid towards Quennet Copse and Ruby Wood. The 24th Division was unaffected by the German counter-stroke on 30 November, but its forward units did send back several intelligence reports indicating increased enemy activity in Bellicourt.

Whenever conditions allowed, working parties were employed on improving the defences and accommodation. The 8/West Kent expended a considerable amount of time and energy converting the chalk quarry known as The Egg into a comfortable Battalion HQ. Working parties from 177 Brigade excavated and fitted out another rather superior dugout known as the Leicester Lounge. This relatively salubrious shelter lay near to the disintegrating remains of an old steam engine, known familiarly as the 'leave train'. Although peace and quiet were appreciated by all, 3/RB thought the Germans were becoming a little too friendly when they erected a board wishing the RB 'Merry Christmas'. A Lewis was immediately turned on the sign and shot it down. The battalion was not however averse to a degree of cultural distraction. In February 1918 its diarist noted with some pleasure that the battalion's string band had been reinforced by the addition of three new players. Riflemen Breedon, Fawcett and Pollock were respectively late of the Drury Lane Theatre, the Scottish Symphony Orchestra and the Trocadero Hotel.

One of the most popular pastimes in the Hargicourt sector was to count the number of rather despondent looking trees comprising Ruby Wood. Frequently, messages arrived at Brigade and Divisional HQ which claimed that the wood was daily growing or reducing. Some trees were reputed to be made of tempered steel and capable of hiding a battalion of evil intentioned snipers. The 'wonderful wood'(7) maintained its fascination for troops of 72 Brigade until its units left the area. In an attempt to solve and photograph the mystery, one of its members returned to the site in 1919. By that time all evidence of the wood had entirely disappeared.[8]

The 24th Division was relieved in late February by the 66th. The West Kents claimed that 'we all had very pleasant memories of the Hargicourt sector',[9] a sentiment no doubt appreciated by the incoming second line Territorials who had experienced a very difficult time at Passchendaele. Malakoff Farm, Cologne Farm and the area to the east of Villeret was developed into the division's Forward Zone. On the insistence of the recently appointed Divisional General, each of the three brigades maintained one full battalion in the Forward Zone, one in the Battle Zone and one in support. On 21 March, companies of the 2/5 Manchester garrisoned the quarries and posts around Cologne Farm. The first Battalion HQ knew of the attack was the arrival of a breathless cook announcing that the Germans were through to the rear. Those Manchesters who survived the initial onslaught escaped to the Battle Zone behind the village. This battalion fared only marginally better than the 2/8 Lancashire Fusiliers which occupied Malakoff Farm and the 2/5 East Lancashire which manned the approaches to Villeret. German grenades were bouncing down dugout steps before the Fusiliers and the East Lancs knew the battle had begun.

Ten platoons of the 2/7 Lancashire Fusiliers and two companies of the divisional Pioneers were in occupation of Templeux Quarries on the morning of 21 March. The 5/Border had only been converted to Pioneers in February and had not yet suffered the drain of experienced and physically fit infantry common to many other Pioneer units. Having spent three years with the Northumbrian Division, it had a strong and proud reputation as a fighting battalion. By 11.00am, A and B Companies were surrounded but they fought on until 2.30pm. Even then, small isolated posts held out east of Templeux village until they too were swept away. Only three officers and 80 men of the two forward companies escaped back to join the third which, by that time, had moved up to the west of Templeux from Roisel. Little is known of what happened to the Fusilier platoons. A fatality list of 87, a slightly higher number than that of the Pioneers, suggests that they too put up

A British soldier poses for the camera in a captured German trench near Cologne Farm. Trenches in this sector were notoriously wet.

Allied cooperation at a Hargicourt YMCA. Australian, American and British troops enjoy its spartan facilities. IWM E3401

a substantial resistance.

In September 1918, with 230 Brigade leading the way, the 74th Division was allocated the responsibility for taking Templeux-le-Guérard. The 15/Suffolk and 16/Sussex cleared the quarries and occupied positions north of Hargicourt on 18 September. Australian 1 Brigade next took the van and continued on into the village itself. Standing walls and piles of rubble three to four feet in height provided the defenders with additional cover, but the 4th Battalion pushed on, cleared the ruins and dug in about 400m to the east of the village. Cologne Farm once again lived up to its bloody reputation, remaining uncaptured until a tank waddled up to assist the 1st Battalion. Another tank supported the attack of the 9th Battalion in Villeret, while the 3rd Battalion assaulted the northern part of the Cologne Spur. This unit attacked through what was supposedly the 74th Division's area, swept over Hussar Post and linked up with the 10/Buffs near Malakoff Farm. A combination of stiffening German resistance, especially around Quennemont Farm, and the numerical weakness of Australian battalions conspired to slow the advance and make it impossible for the momentum to carry it forward to the Hindenburg Line.

With Hargicourt and Villeret cleared, the next objective was the Hindenburg outpost line. British and Dominion troops held approximately the same positions as those reached by the 34th and 35th Divisions 13 months earlier. Australian brigades were desperately under-strength and in need of a rest. On 21 September the 1st Battalion was relieved and assembled for a hot meal in a sunken road to the south of Hargicourt. Its deserved period of rest was shattered when orders arrived instructing the battalion to return to the line for another attack. One hundred and nineteen men refused to move. They argued that they were being used too often as assault troops and that British units were not shouldering their share of the burden. All the protesters were arrested and charged with desertion rather than mutiny; with one exception they were subsequently found guilty. Fortunately, the arrival of peace relieved the authorities of enforcing punishment.

Notes

1. H.Stacke, *The Worcestershire Regiment in the Great War*, p.248
2. A.Horne, *The Diary of a World War I Cavalry Officer*, 3 June 1917. IWM Dept. of Documents.
3. Ibid, 3 July 1917
4. J.Ewing, *The Royal Scots 1914-18*, p.468
5. War Diary of 11/Suffolk, 26 August 1917. WO.95.2458
6. *The History of the 8th Queen's Own Royal West Kent,* (no author) p.133
7. Ibid, p.144
8. Some maps of 1918 show a feature called 'Twelve Trees' a few metres to the south of Ruby Wood.
9. *The History of the 8th Queen's Own Royal West Kent,* p.152

Hargicourt today

Templeux Quarries are out of bounds to the public and dangerous to enter. There are many unstable craters and mounds of spoil to trap the unwary and unwelcome visitor. The village of Templeux-le-Guérard itself is really in two parts. The northern sector nestles beneath the quarries, includes the communal cemetery extension and supports a bar. The more substantial southern portion is gathered around the war memorial and church.

The D6E to Hargicourt has Templeux-le-Guérard British Cemetery on its northern side. Above it, trees surround the mounds of Templeux Quarries **(2)** and, further along on the southern side, the workings of Hargicourt Quarries scar the fields. Tucked beneath the southern bank of the D6E is Hargicourt British Cemetery. Hargicourt Communal Extension lies on a lane on the east side of the village.

Hargicourt village has a corner shop, a PTT and the inevitable boule pit. Slag Quarry has been filled in, the only remains today being the tell-tale mounds beside derelict buildings. Unnamed Farm has disappeared, while Cologne Farm on the crest has an air of disinterest and decay. Ruby Farm is now beneath the motorway, but the site of Malakoff Farm **(3)** is just to its east between the Bellicourt and Bony roads. The old sugar refinery was rebuilt a little to the south and now again lies abandoned close to Ruby Wood. Malakoff Wood can be reached up a long track. Apart from quiet, a suspicious lump of concrete and a few holes in the ground, it has nothing to visit.

Villeret straggles up the D57 to meet Hargicourt's outlying houses. In recent years it used to boast a shop but the owner gave up the unequal struggle and it has now been modernised as a house. The village's chief feature is a rather forlorn water tower on what the British

The immaculate little Hargicourt Communal Cemetery Extension looks over Hargicourt Valley and up to the Cologne Ridge beyond.

In memory of when fighting again swept through Templeux le-Guérard, this plaque hangs on a wall at the western end of the village. (12)

called Maxim Road. It sits disconsolately atop the ridge and is a useful landmark. **(4)** The site of Fervaque Farm is now occupied by a copse. On the spur to the north-west of the village is a memorial cross to Lieutenant-Colonel Wrenford, OC of the 4/East Lancashire. He was killed near the spot on 21 March and the memorial was erected by his family in the post-war years. Although Wrenford's remains were later found, identified and taken to Cabaret Rouge British Cemetery for burial, the cross remained in place. It was neglected for many years but has recently been restored. Villeret Churchyard Cemetery is on the west side of the village.

Tour of Hargicourt
(Tour Map 7)
13.7kms, 8.5miles. 3.75 hours

Park at the northern end of Templeux-le-Guérard near the café in the *Place Francois Mitterand*. Take the D6 towards Ronssoy and after 70m fork right towards the communal cemetery. **(1)** The British plot is to the north of the civilian graves and offers good views across the valley towards Ronssoy. Return to the café and take the D6E towards Hargicourt. Templeux British Cemetery is on the left after 800m. Take the track to the left immediately after the cemetery. This climbs up passing Templeux Quarries and reaches the plateau beyond. Continue along until you join the Ronssoy–Hargicourt road near the squat water tower. Turn right towards Hargicourt. Take the grass track on the left

Taken about half way across No Man's Land, this shot shows the ground over which the 11/Suffolk and the 10/Lincoln attacked on 26 August 1917. The motorway embankment is artificial but the slope up to the Cologne Ridge is easily seen.

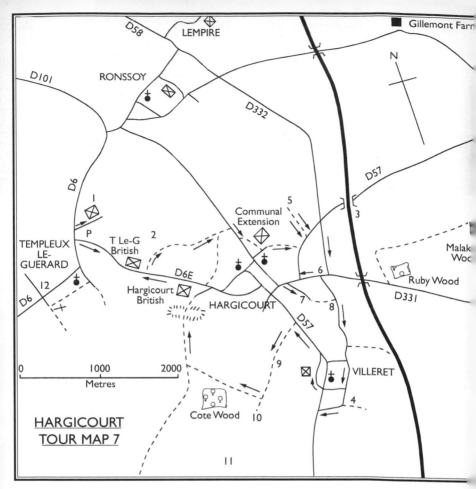

HARGICOURT TOUR MAP 7

Map labels: D58, LEMPIRE, Gillemont Farm, D101, RONSSOY, D332, D6, D57, 1, P, 2, TEMPLEUX LE-GUERARD, T Le-G British, D6E, Communal Extension, 5, 3, Malak Woo, Ruby Wood, 6, 12, D6, Hargicourt British, HARGICOURT, 7, 8, D331, D57, 9, VILLERET, Cote Wood, 10, 4, 11, N

Scale: 0 — 1000 — 2000 Metres

Cologne Farm, rebuilt only a few yards from its original site, is once again in ruins.

Nestled among the disused workings of Hargicourt Quarries lies the British cemetery. Sunday 'hunters' often use the shelter and wall of the cemetery as cover while shooting into the quarries.

after 400m (just as the houses begin) and follow round to Hargicourt Communal Extension. 80m after the cemetery, turn left onto a minor road.

This joins the D57. Turn left and head towards the motorway. A short excursion up the track to the left goes climbs to the site of Hussar and Artaxerxes Posts. **(5)** At the junction before the motorway, turn right and walk up the road which runs parallel to the motorway. Take the road towards Hargicourt after 250m. The junction of a minor road from the left and a track to the right was the site of Unnamed Farm. **(6)** Look north and east. Ruby Wood and the site of Malakoff Farm are on the other side of the motorway.

Continue towards Hargicourt and after 400m turn sharp left onto *Rue de l'Usine*. This road climbs up past the site of Slag Quarry **(7)**. Beyond the derelict buildings, the road becomes a path. Continue along, bear left and it joins the minor road to Villeret at Cologne Farm. **(8)** Turn right and drop down towards Villeret. The road crosses the path of the old railway; New and Club Quarries were in the fields to the

High on the slope above Hargicourt stands Wrenford Cross. Lieutenant Colonel Wrenford was attached to the 4/East Lancs from the Worcester Regiment. The cross stands near to the site of his battalion's HQ dugout.

117

The original inscription on the cross records that Wrenford was buried in an unknown grave. The later addition, which notes that his remains were eventually identified and taken elsewhere, has not withstood the ravages of time with quite so much resolve.

right. In Villeret, head south behind the church and make your way to the water tower. **(4)** This position gives good views across the motorway towards Quarry Wood and the Cologne and Buisson Ridges.

Head back to the main road and turn north. Take *Rue Neuve* (left) in the village and follow round to the communal cemetery. Rejoin the main road and continue north. After 800m and just before the road reaches the valley bottom south of Hargicourt, take a track which comes in from the left opposite a house with green railings and copper beeches. This climbs up past Bob Quarry **(9)** to Colonel Wrenford's memorial. **(10)** The copse 400m further on to the south marks the position of Fervaque Farm. **(11)** Zulu and Kaffir Copses can be seen to the south-east. Turn around to face the direction from which you have just walked, take the grass track on the left and drop down past Cote Wood. This headland joins the old Jeancourt-Hargicourt road. Turn right and continue on to Hargicourt British Cemetery. Immediately south of the cemetery the track passes between Higson's Quarries. These were used extensively by HQ staff and support companies. Return to the track and rejoin the D6E. Turn left and walk back to Templeux.

Chapter Eight

HESBECOURT AND JEANCOURT

On 27 August 1914, a small party of 1/Warwicks under the command of Major Poole, spent a hungry and uncomfortable night in a sunken lane near Hesbécourt. The following morning, the party, which included Lieutenant (later Field Marshall) B.L.Montgomery, continued its search for the rest of the 4th Division. It marched through Jeancourt and on to Péronne.

Nearly two years later, during the cold, wet month of May 1917, British III Corps followed the Germans' retreat towards their prepared positions near the St Quentin Canal. Although the names of woods and villages were marked on British maps, there was little to distinguish one piece of straggling undergrowth or one heap of rubble from another. 177 Brigade of the 59th Division approached two such mounds on 31 March. Divisional artillery pounded the former sites of Hesbécourt and Hervilly before the 2/5 Leicester and 2/4 Lincoln moved forward to take them. There was little German opposition and the Leicesters pushed on to occupy the high ground of Hill 140 to the east. On their right flank, 178 Brigade captured Vendelles and Jeancourt, although the 2/6 and 2/8 Sherwood Foresters were temporarily forced to evacuate their positions in the latter village until the high ground above was secured.

There were few standing walls in any of the three villages. British troops discovered evidence of a German field hospital in Jeancourt and the graves of two British airmen in Hesbécourt. There were still plenty of cellars and after a search for booby traps, the wet and weary troops

A rear-guard machine-gun post covering the advancing Allied troops as the Germans withdrew in March, 1917, to the Hindenburg Line.

The ruins of Jeancourt's sugar factory following its capture on 31 March 1917.

sought what shelter they could. With Vendelles and Roisel secured, Hervilly was safe save from large calibre howitzers. Railways were already being pushed forward towards Montigny, and Hervilly rapidly became a place of concentration and assembly. Hesbécourt and Jeancourt were not so fortunate. Overlooked by high ground, they could not be secured until the heights dominated by Fervaque Farm, Grand Priel Woods and the village of Le Verguier were cleared.

The 2/4 Leicester was the unfortunate battalion chosen to make the first effort against the farm. Despite several attempts, dense wire and heavy fire prevented any substantial progress. On 3 April it was the turn of 2/4 Lincoln. It too failed, as did later assaults. Attempts to outflank the farm through Grand Priel Woods were also frustrated. Eventually, a week after the attacks began, the Germans voluntarily withdrew from the farm. The site and the nearby woods were occupied by 176 and 177 Brigades; Hesbécourt and Jeancourt immediately became support and billeting areas. Working parties left nightly to dig and wire new positions on the slopes above the two villages. Quarries in and around Jeancourt were converted to battalion HQs, while Hervilly was developed into a brigade HQ. The existing German cemetery in Jeancourt was extended to accommodate the fallen of the 59th Division, and branches of a light railway were pushed up from Montigny sidings to both villages. Shielded by the hills, field ambulances and howitzer batteries moved into the fields and hutted camps appeared in the valleys to the west. Work on improving the trenches continued during occupation of the villages by the 34th, 35th and 24th Divisions and the Cavalry Corps. The British cemetery was kept in constant use by the addition of men lost during the normal routine of trench warfare and from those who perished in trench raids.

In March 1918, with the 24th Division to its right and the 16th on its left, the 66th Division was responsible for the area's defence. The three battalions in the Forward Zone were immediately overrun and the enemy pressed on to the Battle Zone. Reserve battalions of each brigade which had been resting to the rear of the Battle Zone suffered from enemy shelling as they moved up to their alarm positions from Montigny, Hervilly and Hesbécourt. As the enemy poured over the skyline above the quarries, a battery of 18-pounder guns covering the withdrawal of the 6/LF to the higher ground south and west of Templeux-le-Guérard, fired from a position near the village crucifix. On their right the 2/6 and 2/7 Manchester held Cote Wood, Brosse Woods and Fervaque Farm. These battalions delayed the Germans until late in the afternoon when the attackers finally cleared the farm with *flammenwerfer* fire. Battalion HQ of the 2/6 Manchester then withdrew to Carpeza Copse on the slopes behind the farm and held that position during the night. Fire from Carpeza halted the German thrust down the minor road between Jeancourt and Hargicourt. Until they could bring artillery forward to deal with the redoubts at the rear of the

The fields around Hervilly were used by the Germans as an aerodrome in 1915 and 1916. RFC aircraft bombed the village and airfield on several occasions. When they withdrew in March 1917, the Germans completed the destruction of the already heavily damaged church.

Battle Zone, the German advance would make little further progress.

Further along the crest, the 4/East Lancashire was having an equally torrid time. Enemy troops climbed the slopes west of Hargicourt and Villeret, killed most of the battalion's senior officers, including Lieutenant-Colonel Wrenford and Major Bolton, and pushed along the spur above Jeancourt. A rearguard under the command of Captain Bolton delayed the Germans for a time but, when in danger of envelopment, its three officers and 90 men withdrew on Hesbécourt. The reserve battalion of 73 Brigade was sent from its divisional area to support the East Lancashire Division. The 9/Sussex hastily positioned itself in four very inadequate redoubts east of Hesbécourt. Although some trenches were only one foot deep, the garrisons were well supplied with rations and SAA. Trinity and Trinket redoubts were well wired and lay on reverse slopes about 600m apart. Carpeza Copse lay another 500m to the south of Trinket. Two other redoubts, Upstart and Trifle, were respectively sited on the spur overlooking Carpeza and a few hundred yards behind Trinity.

German shells began to land on the Sussex during the night and at 6.00am on 22 March infantry began to encroach upon Trinity and Trinket. Their garrisons repulsed several assaults and were even reinforced by a party of the 2/6 Manchester under Captain Collier which had been forced from Carpeza Copse. Premature reports of the fall of both redoubts were fed back to Battalion HQ in Hesbécourt but, in the end, weight of numbers told. The defence of Trinity and Trinket delayed the enemy for nearly 24 hours. Unsupported by artillery and with the right flank hopelessly exposed by the fall of Fervaque Farm **(8)**, the garrisons apparently 'just stuck it out until further resistance was hopeless'.[1] A few men of A Company escaped to Trifle but Captain Saxon and the remainder of C Company surrendered and were soon put to work clearing the battlefield.

At least one squadron of the 9/Lancers, the 15th Entrenching Battalion and two tanks were sent up to Hervilly Wood to support the Sussex and the Manchesters; this party was later joined by the band, servants and orderly room staff of the 5/Border. The Entrenching Battalion (which according to one officer of the 9/Sussex, 'fought like devils'[2] was the new name for the recently disbanded 10/LNL. D Company of the Sussex in Upstart redoubt was outflanked and the survivors fell back to the cavalry lining White Chalk Trench near a light railway. 198 Brigade had been pushed from Jeancourt and it was evident that troops of the 7/Northants manning four redoubts between that village and Vendelles, were coming under increasing pressure.

A small shrine and a few bricks mark the site of Jeancourt church in September 1918.

Having failed to discover the whereabouts of 17 Brigade HQ, the Northants' colonel sent a message to 73 Brigade at Bernes reporting that as both his flanks were in the air, he felt compelled to retire. The Northants fell back to cover the ground Vendelles-Montigny-Hervilly. Here they were joined by an assortment of other troops which included 9/Sussex, the Entrenching Battalion and 2/7 Manchester. The enemy was also through on the division's left flank, the 6/LF having been

The rebuilt church at Jeancourt has the revolutionary slogan 'Liberté, Fraternité, Égalité' inscribed above its main entrance. The communal cemetery and the British extension lie at the far end of the road.

unable to prevent a German debouchment from George's Copse (6) north of the Roisel-Templeux road. Despite the Germans affording excellent targets to D Company positioned near the crucifix, the Fusiliers withdrew to Roisel where they plundered an abandoned BEF canteen for rations. The battalion then fell back on Nobescourt Farm. (7)

September 1918

Once the battle had moved west, the Germans and their prisoners had a lot of burying to do. By September, when Australian forces appeared in front of Jeancourt, the British cemetery had been considerably enlarged. On 10 September Jeancourt was deserted and 1 Australian Brigade passed through, pushing back a few enemy posts east of Hesbécourt and retaking the former sites of Trinity and Trinket redoubts. As an attempt to advance over the crest was halted by fire from Templeux and Hargicourt, the Dominion troops withdrew to some dead ground and regrouped. Time was needed to prepare for the next assault, and this eventually took place on 18 September. The 11th and 12th Battalions advanced towards Fervaque Farm, meeting with little resistance until a nest of machine guns opened up from Carpeza Copse. The scrub was rushed and a substantial bag of prisoners collected. The 12th Battalion took the former Manchesters' positions in Brosse Woods, but further east in Grand Priel Woods, the advance was delayed by fire from a German HQ in the chateau grounds. With companies of well under one hundred, the 11th Battalion fought its way through the woods, emerging from its shattered trunks to come under yet more fire. Firing Lewis guns from the hip, the Australians charged up the slope to Caution Dugouts, south-west of Villeret. Away to the north the 74th Division had advanced through George's Copse and across Templeux Quarries towards Hargicourt.

The recapture of the land lost by the East Lancashire Division had been a bloody process. The Australians lost heavily and Jeancourt

The badly battered centre of Roisel soon after the war ended. The capture of the town and its important rail links was a crucial factor in the period prior to the assault on the Hindenburg Line.

cemetery was once again extended. Field ambulances and artillery moved back under the shelter of the ridges and the light railway was relaid. Roads were repaired, craters filled and troops again plodded up and over the slopes to Hargicourt and the Hindenburg Line beyond.

Notes

1. War Diary of 9/Sussex, 22 March 1918. WO.95.2219
2. Ibid. Report by Captain Saxon.

Hesbécourt and Jeancourt today

The 30 or so houses and farms which constitute Hesbécourt straggle either side of the D6E. Apart from the communal cemetery, it has little to recommend it as a tourist attraction. The valley and fields to the east are open and in summer exposed to what is sometimes a fierce sun. A long track leads past Carpeza Copse, ending near Trinket Copse. Amid the bushes and shrubs which now grow on the site is a substantial memorial. It was erected in the 1930s to commemorate Protestants who met to worship there in the 17th century.

Hervilly is a much more attractive village, possessing a particularly well-kept farm near the junction of its two roads. A German aerodrome occupied the flat fields to its west. An unmade road leaves the D24 to pass between Hervilly Wood and Cross Wood, joining the D31 west of Jeancourt. While most French villages usually appear deserted,

The graves of Captain Cruikshank DSO, MC and Lieutenant Preston MC in Hesbécourt Communal Cemetery. The two men were members of 20 Squadron, and crewed one of the four planes lost by the squadron on 15 September 1916. The night before his death, Cruikshank is reported to have said he would rather get Boelcke than a VC.

Jeancourt is a positive ghost town. It has a reasonable collection of houses and farms, two churches and a large British and German cemetery.

On the hill above Jeancourt and Montigny, the latter being little more than a disused railway station and a large expanse of scruffy ground, is Vendelles. This village was used extensively by the British as a rest area. A number of graves of the 59th Division were later removed but there remain five of the division and an Australian sergeant of the 4th Pioneer Battalion in the communal cemetery. Although the scenery is not spectacular, a drive through these villages, which remained behind the lines from April 1917 until March 1918, is a pleasant and relaxing experience.

Tour of Hesbécourt and Jeancourt
(Tour Map 8)
15kms, 9.3miles. 3.5 hours

Park at Hesbécourt and visit the communal cemetery behind the church. Walk down the main street and turn right to Hervilly. White Chalk Trench and the light railway **(5)** ran along the fields on your left. At the D24 turn left and after 400m take the minor road on the left. This track passes south of Hervilly Wood and joins the D31 west of Jeancourt. Jeancourt Communal Extension Cemetery is on the west side of the village, south of the D31.

Walk to the centre of the village, turn left at the war memorial and after 120m turn right onto *Rue Fervaque*. If the crops are still in the fields do not take this small road but keep to the main road and walk back to Hesbécourt. This route passes a water tower and at its summit gives good views along the valley leading up to the site of Trinket **(2)** and Trinity **(1)** redoubts and the high ground above Hargicourt. Upstart

German and British headstones beneath the Cross of Sacrifice in Jeancourt Communal Cemetery Extension.

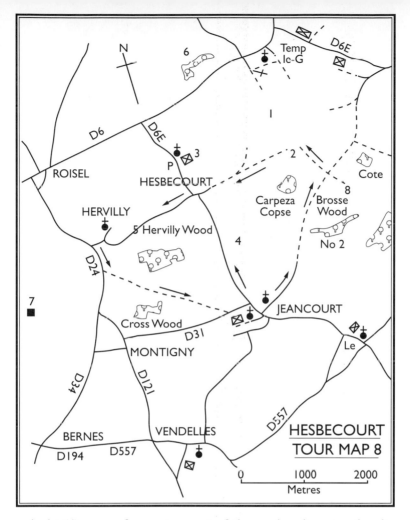

redoubt **(4)** was a few metres east of the road as it approaches its summit, while Trifle **(3)** was on the slope east of Hesbécourt communal cemetery. (9kms, 5.6miles, 2 hours)

If the crops are down, take *Rue Fervaque*. This road, which is marked on Michelin maps, starts off well but becomes very patchy. It climbs gently, with Brosse Woods No.2 and No.1 on its eastern side.

On the crest (3000m) there is (sometimes) a junction of tracks. Occasionally, they can be ploughed out of existence. Take the left one. The small copse on your left marks the site of Trinket redoubt. Keeping to the edge of the field, cross to the copse. At its western end a track begins. This passes Carpeza Copse (on your left) and follows the length of the valley back to Hesbécourt.

Chapter Nine

CEMETERIES IN THE RIQUEVAL AREA

(The plot, row and grave number of certain individuals are indicated)

Beaumetz Communal Cemetery

Lying 600m south of the D194 between Cartigny and Hancourt, this tiny cemetery contains the graves of four RFC men. They were the crews of two Morane BBs from 60 Squadron, shot down on 2 August 1916. One of the pilots was Sergeant A.Walker, who had Second Lieutenant Clark, attached from the RHA, as his observer. Clark apparently fell out of the damaged aircraft as it spun out of control. Lieutenant Ormsby's headstone indicates that he was attached from Eaton's Motor MG Corps, a Canadian unit. His observer, Henry Newton, formerly of the Rangers and the Cheshire Regiment, had only just joined the squadron.

At the time, the squadron believed the planes had been brought down by ack-ack fire, but it is more likely that they were victims of Kampfeinsitzer staffeln Vaux, a small unit operating Fokker *Eindekkers.* Ormsby and Newton were *Leutnant* Kurt Wintgen's thirteenth kill, while Walker and Clark were Leutnant Wilhelm Frankl's seventh. Before they were themselves eventually killed, both German pilots were awarded the *Pour le Merité,* and claimed 19 and 20 kills

Germans gather round the wreckage of a British aircraft. The bodies of two airmen lie in the foreground.

respectively. The day after the two Moranes were lost, 60 Squadron lost its seventh aircraft since arriving in France. Trenchard then pulled it out of the line; the only time a RFC squadron was withdrawn from operations.

Berthaucourt Communal Cemetery
This cemetery is sited on the D73 to Maissemy. There are four British burials near the gate close to some local paupers' graves. The main British plot is further in. Three rows contain the graves of 1st Division soldiers killed during the advance on the village. The middle row comprises 16 2/KRRC, mainly of 18 September. One man is from the Queen Victoria's, who like many of 1918's, dead has the badge of his original regiment on his headstone rather than the one to which he had been posted. The rear row is largely Northamptons of 24 September, while the front is formed of 22 men of the 2/Sussex killed near Essling redoubt also on 24 September. Among the fallen, who lie almost within a stone's throw of where they died, are Captain Geoffrey Sunderland and Second Lieutenant Fred Adkin MM.

Bouvincourt Communal Cemetery
An attractive village, whose cemetery lies between it and the D944. Five British soldiers were buried by Field Ambulances and another, Private John Morgan of the 1/4 East Yorks, by the enemy.

Buire Communal Cemetery
This contains eight soldiers, six of whom are Australians. The other two are gunners from D Battery, 86 Brigade RFA, killed on 22 March 1918.

Calvaire Cemetery, Montbrehain
On the northwest side of the village, this cemetery contains the graves of 48 Australians, mainly of the 24th Battalion, and 20 UK soldiers. Thirteen of the dead are unidentified. The Australians attacked the village from the north-west between 3–5 October as the Sherwood Foresters approached it from the south and west. The graves include those of Sergeant Reginald Davies, DCM, *Medaille Militaire* of the 17th Battalion and five men of the 2nd (Australian) Pioneers, all killed on 5 October. One of them, Sergeant Eric Read from Queensland, had the MM and *Croix* de Guerre. In row D are the remains of J.Pamphilon of the 6th Battalion Tank Corps. Pamphilon apparently enlisted in the Queen Victoria's Rifles in 1914 aged 15, later transferred to the RAF and finally ended up in the Tank Corps. He was killed on 8 October.

One soldier of the 2/R.Inniskilling Fusiliers buried by the Germans in September 1914 lies in the communal cemetery a few yards to the north.

Chapelle British Cemetery, Holnon
This concentration cemetery, a pleasant oasis of shrubs and rose bushes, lies 50 metres south of the N29. It contains the remains of 600 soldiers, a good proportion of whom came from the West Yorkshire, DLI, Leicester, Notts & Derby and Norfolk Regiments, killed in September 1918. These men died

Hancourt British Cemetery. The graves of over 20 men of the 1/4 East Yorks, killed as they withdrew through the area in March 1918, are on the right.

during the assaults on the village and the Quadrilateral. There is also a number of known and unknown men of the Ox & Bucks and Worcesters who were defending Ellis and Enghien redoubts, and soldiers of the 33rd, 35th and 59th Divisions who died in the vicinity during March and April 1917. Almost 45% of the graves are unnamed.

Doingt Communal Cemetery Extension

This village lies east of the D944, south-east of Péronne. It was captured by the 5th Australian Division in early September 1918. Three CCS, the 20th, 41st and 55th, established themselves here between September and October. The British Extension is nicely shaded and has an open aspect to the north. It contains the remains of soldiers largely from the 12th, 18th, 74th Divisions and several men of the reconstituted 2/Munster. Over 100 US troops who also died of wounds were later removed. Major Reginald Fillingham RGA, MC and Bar, who had enlisted as a ranker aged 14 in 1904, died here of wounds received at Ste Emilie.

Hancourt British Cemetery

A small cemetery of under 120 graves lying 100m along a farm track to the east of the village. It was begun by the Australians in September 1918 and later enlarged by the concentration of graves from the area around Estrées-en-Chaussée. Many of the graves are those of men from the 50th Division, including nearly two dozen from the 1/4 East Yorks. The CO of the 16/LF, Lieutenant-Colonel Stone DSO, was buried here in early October. Many of his men lie further east in cemeteries near Joncourt.

Hargicourt British Cemetery

This neat, liberally proportioned cemetery with a good aspect over the hills to the south, contains the remains of over 300 British and Indian soldiers. It was used mainly by the 34th and 35th Divisions in 1917 and contains many of their men killed during the attacks on the Cologne Ridge. Among them is Corporal Matthew Whelan DCM, MM of the 26/NF. There are also cavalry from late 1917 and many of the 24th Division from early 1918. Several unknown Rifle Brigade, probably of the 3rd Battalion killed near Cooker Quarry, lie within its flint walls. Second Lieutenant Henry Dunn, Battalion Intelligence Officer of the 8/West Kent, apparently a very adventurous young man who spent much of his time wandering around No Man's Land, was sniped and buried here. (I.H.4) Major Harold Paris MC and Sergeant Reg Taylor MM, both of the 138th Heavy Battery RGA, lie together a little apart from the main plot. (I.J.1,2) Paris had gone to France as a subaltern in August 1914. He and Taylor were killed on 6 October 1918. The Sikh troops, as is common to men of their religion, do not have the date of death inscribed on their memorial.

Hargicourt Communal Cemetery Extension

A small, compact cemetery, the communal extension has 73 British and Australian burials. It now lies isolated from the village's Protestant cemetery because the German troops buried in the space between were later removed. It has men from the 10/Lincoln, 11/Suffolk, 15th and 16/Royal Scots killed during the attacks near Ruby Farm in August 1917. Some Worcesters of October and Australians and East Kents of 21 September complete this secluded little cemetery.

Hesbécourt Communal Cemetery

The cemetery has 14 British and Australian burials in several plots. Captain Guy Cruikshank DSO, MC and his observer Lieutenant Rudolph Preston MC were shot down by Oswald Boelcke in mid-September 1916. Cruikshank was a well-known figure in the RFC having, among other activities, been involved in some earlier cloak and dagger work. In April 1915 he had formed a special flight for dropping spies behind enemy lines and, after flying such an operation in September of that year, was awarded his DSO. Piloting a Sopwith, he and Preston were shot down by Boelcke somewhere between Ytres and Havrincourt Wood. Boelcke was leading the newly formed *Jagestaffel 2* and personally claimed two kills that day. Private Fred Cole of the 9/Sussex was probably wounded in one of the nearby redoubts and subsequently buried by the Germans. The remainder include two Australians from September 1918 and a King's Dragoon Guard of May 1917. Another 28 men of the 59th Division and

35 Australians were removed from the adjoining extension and reburied at Roisel.

High Tree Cemetery, Montbrehain
A small cemetery to the east of the village, nor far from the site of Doon mill and copse, containing 48 graves. Besides four Australians, most of the remainder are soldiers of the 6th Division: 1/KSLI, 1/Buffs and 9/Norfolks killed on 8 October.

Jeancourt Communal Cemetery Extension
There were already over 150 Germans buried in the extension when the British arrived in late March 1917. The 59th Division immediately began to use the site and it remained operational until March 1918. After the armistice, 369 fatalities of March and September were concentrated into the cemetery. There are now nearly 500 burials. These include a good number of Manchesters, 10/LNL and 3/RB of 21 March. Like most disbanded battalions, the dead of the Loyals, who by March had officially become the 15th Entrenching Battalion, are listed in the Soldiers Died rolls of their former regiment and have its badge on their headstones.

The 18 September battle is represented by Australians, largely of the 12th, 13th and 16th Battalions. Lieutenant McGuire of the 13th Battalion was a commissioned ranker who won both the MC and MM. (II.A.31) The remainder reflect the regiments line-holding in the sector during 1917. There are men of the 35th Division, for example RSM Hodson MC of the 21/NF, (II.D.10) and a wide assortment of cavalry. These range from the Queen's Bays, Fort Garry Horse, Royal Canadian Dragoons to Lord Strathcona's Horse. One of the more unusual burials is that of Private Reading, 4/Duke of Wellington's. (II.A) Reading, whose name does not appear in the original register, died on 20 December 1915. At that time his battalion was at Ypres so he was presumably a prisoner who died in German hands. His grave, wherever it was originally, was later concentrated into Jeancourt.

Joncourt British Cemetery
Lying immediately west of the Beaurevoir Line and just over the old railway cutting on the Levergies road (D71) this group of 61 burials is predominently comprised of soldiers from the 10/A&SH. Most of these were killed in the attacks on the German defences on 30 September. Among the Argylls is a commissioned ranker, Second Lieutenant Graham Duncan DCM (A1) attached from the 7th Battalion. Another notable casualty is that of Arthur Humphries. (B20) Humphries, a regular with the 2/SWB was attached to the Territorial 1/Monmouth as RSM. He was the holder of the Long Service and Good Conduct medals.

Joncourt Communal Cemetery
Three of the five British graves are those of British aircrew buried by the Germans. Captain Charles Graves of the Nova Scotia Regiment and 9 Squadron RFC was killed in 'bloody April' 1917. His BE2e was one of three sent

on a bombing mission without observers. Although the squadron believed all three had fallen to anti-aircraft fire, it seems likely that they were victims of Otto Bernert of *Jasta Boelcke*. Bernert had the staggering success to shoot down not only these three aircraft but also two others all within twenty minutes of each other. He had been awarded the *Pour le Merité* the previous day, wore glasses and, owing to a bayonet wound, had a virtually useless left arm!

Captain A Field and Second Lieutenant Walter Smith of 49 Squadron (the orginal register has Field in 48 Squadron) were on a photographic mission between Cambrai and St Quentin on 9 January 1918. Their Bristol Fighter was shot down over Nauroy by Kurt Ungewitter of *Schusta 5*.

For some unknown reason Private A.Bacon of the 6/SF was buried here rather than with his comrades who fell on the same day at Ramicourt.

Joncourt East British Cemetery

Access to this battlefield cemetery is down a track which can, in wet weather, bear more of a resemblance to a stream. Neatly tucked away admidst the corn and beet fields it contains the remains of 71 men all killed between 30 September and 3 October. Of the total, 62 are either 15 or 16/LF or 2/Manchester. There is one soldier of the Sherwood Foresters' Brigade, Private J.Smith of the 8th Battalion and three troopers of the 20/Hussars. These men, whose unit tried to push through a gap created in the Beaurevoir Line by the Manchesters lie togther in row A

La Baraque British Cemetery

It is a small neat cemetery with the graves of 60 gunners, machine-gunners, infantry and medical personnel, largely of the 46th and 32nd Divisions. The seven medical orderlies were from the 91st and 92nd Field Ambulances, killed during a German air raid on the night of 30 September. Three men were brought into the cemetery from Pontru churchyard seven years after the armistice.

Levergies Communal Cemetery

One identified RAF pilot and 13 soldiers lie in this typically French communal cemetery. Eleven of the 13 are members of the 6/North Stafford killed 3–4 October while attacking Mannequin Hill.

Maissemy German Cemetery

This sombre collection of iron crosses and occasional Jewish headstones contains 15,478 graves from between 1916-1918, including nearly 8000 in a mass grave. Like most German cemeteries, it has a fairly gloomy and melancholy aspect.

Marteville Communal Cemetery

Artillery units of the 35th Division began burying here in April 1917. It was used again after March 1918. There are several troops of the 17/West Yorks and 19/DLI killed on 1 May 1917 who were attached to 106th TMB. There are a few men of the Black Watch and Cameron Highlanders of September, and Sergeant T.Earl DCM and Bar of the Welch Regiment.

Montbrehain British Cemetery

Some yards south of the old railway crossing on the D283, this cemetery largely contains the graves of Territorials of the Sherwood Foresters who took but could not retain their grip on the village on 3 October. The remainder of the 86 men buried in the two rows are mainly those of the 1/Leicester, 9/Norfolk and a regular battalion of the Foresters, the 2nd. These were units of the 6th Division.

Ramicourt British Cemetery

This cemetery was begun by the 18th Field Ambulance and IX Corps' Burial Officer in early October. It lies just to the east of the Beaurevoir Line. The burials reflect the capture of the village by the Sherwood Foresters' Brigade on 3 October rather than the attack on it by the 16/LF. Thirty-eight of the 97 UK soldiers are from the battalions of the Territorial brigade. These include Lance-Sergeant Wilfred Hunt of the 5th Battalion who was killed on 3 October. Hunt, from Alfreton, enlisted in 1914 at the early age of 16 years, one of five brothers who served. There are also men of the 1/KSLI and the 2/KOYLI (6th and 32nd Divisions respectively) and 18 Australians. Six Pioneers of the 1/Monmouth also lie in this trim cemetery.

Roisel Communal Cemetery Extension

Although by no means a large town, Roisel does have a confusing alignment of roads. The cemetery lies on the road to Villers-Faucon. British units had buried in the communal cemetery from April 1917 and the Germans continued to use it after March 1918. Four CCS arrived at Roisel between October and November and opened the extension. All but one of the graves in the communal were later removed to the extension. After the war a good deal of concentration took place. There are now a little under 900 British and Australian and nearly 500 German graves. Men of the 46th Division were brought in to Roisel from Bernes churchyard and over 60 Australians and soldiers of the 59th Division were reburied from Hesbécourt Communal Cemetery Extension. The divisions which faced the German onslaught in March are well represented. There are Worcesters and Argylls of the 66th Division, including the grave of Second Lieutenant J.Buchan VC.

Sequehart British No.1

This lovely little cemetery lies behind the churchyard and was begun by the 6/SF on 10 October. However, the great majority of the 56 burials are those of the 1/Monmouth. Thirty-four of the Pioneers who were collected from the scene of their attack against machine-gun posts before Méricourt are buried here. They include the Adjutant, Captain William James and a CQMS, F.Thomas. James was killed outright but Lieutenant-Colonel Jenkins, who was along side him at the time, was carried away and died of wounds in a CCS at Tincourt.

Twelve of the remainder are men of the 1/LNL (1 Brigade) killed as they attacked to the south of the Monmouths.

Sequehart British No.2

Slightly larger than its near namesake, No.2 is a little further along the path from the churchyard. It lies on a gentle slope, roughly overlooking the area in which most of its interments were killed. It contains 62 graves, 22 of whom are those of the 5/6 Royal Scots killed during their furious attacks and defence of the village. Their two fellow battalions of 14 Brigade, the 15/HLI and 1/Dorset, are also well represented.

Templeux-le-Guérard Communal Cemetery Extension

There are 118 British burials in the communal extension. It was begun in April 1917 by the 59th Division and was subsequently used by, among others, the 34th Division until October 1917. The Lincolnshire Territorials are well represented and there is a sprinkling of Inniskilling Dragoons and 6/Dragoon Guards. There are several Australians who died as they approached the Hindenburg Line on 29-30 September, and there is also a special memorial to 12 men of the Lancashire Fusiliers and East Lancashire who died in German hands. Their original graves in the German Communal Extension were not later identified.

Templeux-le-Guérard British Cemetery

The D6E to Hargicourt has Templeux-le-Guérard British Cemetery on its northern side. Above it, trees surround the mounds of Templeux Quarries and further along on the southern side, the workings of Hargicourt Quarries scar the fields. The cemetery is nicely laid out and, like the communal extension, it too was begun by the 59th Division in April 1917. Line-holding units used it during the remainder of the year. The graves include men of the 19/DLI and Pioneers of the 19/NF who were killed at the Birdcage in August. It was reopened in September and after the war a considerable amount of concentration took place. Among those brought in were cavalry of the 7/South Irish Horse, over 120 of the 50th Division killed at Gouy in early October and a large number of East Lancashire Territorials of the 42nd Division who were originally buried in the grounds of Ste Emilie chateau. There are 188 unnamed graves among the 757.

The cemetery contains the grave of Major Valentine Fleming DSO, the MP for South Oxon. Fleming, and another officer of the Queen's Own Oxfordshire Hussars, Lieutenant Francis Silvertop, were among the victims of the many attacks on Gillemont Farm.

Tertry Communal Cemetery

An often overlooked collection of 15 cavalry and infantry graves, this little cemetery is on the D202 one mile south of the aerodrome at Estrées-en-Chaussée. There are nine men of the 10/Hussars, and soldiers of the 48th Division.

Tertry Communal Cemetery, like the D202 on which it sits, was until recently shaded by mature trees. The main British plot includes the graves of nine men from the 10/Hussars killed in their billets on 9 March 1918. Tertry was frequently used as a divisional assembly area in 1917 and 1918.

Tincourt New British Cemetery

Ten different British CCS worked at Tincourt between April 1917 and the end of the war. After the armistice, the cemetery was considerably enlarged by the concentration of graves from the neighbourhood and elsewhere. It now has well over 2000 interments. There are Canadians, Australians, South Africans, Indians, Chinese and Guernsey Light Infantry. Only 251 of the total are unknown. Many of the graves belong to soldiers of the units which retreated through the area in March. These include Irish and Leicesters, often buried in closely packed rows with two or more badges on each headstone. There is a large number of men who died after the armistice and also several soldiers of the East Lancashire and Manchester Regiments who were killed on the Somme in 1916. Five gunners of 15th Siege Battery RGA lie together, all killed on 25 September 1917. Their unit was giving covering fire to the 34th and 35th Divisions as they attacked near Hargicourt.

A rare example of the badge of the Queen Victoria's Own Corps of Guides. Major Trail, who was attached to the Jodhpur Lancers, is buried in Tincourt British Cemetery.

136

This memorial, at the junction of the D6 and D184 near Tincourt, remembers the crew of a USAAF B17 which crashed in a nearby field in November 1944. The crippled plane was trying to reach the emergency airstrip at Estrées-en-Chaussée. Four of the crew were killed on the raid or in the crash.

One of the more unusual graves is that of Major R. Trail. Trail was a member of the Queen Victoria's Own Corps of Guides and was attached to the Jodhpur Lancers. He died of wounds received during the Lancers' charge near Epéhy

A German observation post squats beside the now defunct track near Tincourt station. It occupies a rather undignified position adjacent to the village's 'bottle bank'.

on 1 December 1917. (III.D.14) A similar fate befell Lieutenant John Pinney of the 38th King's Own Central India Horse. (III.C.20) This young man had begun the war as a RFC observer and was then attached to the cavalry from the 1/RF. He too died of wounds following the cavalry's attempt to dislodge the Germans east of Epéhy.

Trefcon British Cemetery

Possibly the most beautiful cemetery anywhere on the Western Front, this small collection of graves was made by the 6th and 32nd Divisions in September 1918. It lies on the D34 a little north of Beauvois-en-Vermandois. Nestling between a wood and the wall of the old chateau, it possesses an atmosphere which is quite unique. Most of the almost 300 graves are of men killed between 18-20 September. Four men of the 16th Field Ambulance lie together, as do two gunners of B Battery, 168 Brigade RFA. These men, Arthur Riley and Fred Kiddle, were possibly friends who had enlisted together. Both came from Halifax, both were killed on the same day and have almost identical inscriptions on their headstones. This most stunning of cemeteries is infrequently visited.

Uplands Cemetery

Lying on the small road between Magny-la-Fosse and Joncourt this simple cemetery of two rows contains 43 soldiers killed between 29 September and 12 October. Thirty-four of them were from the 15/LF who died while attacking Joncourt. One of them is Corporal A.Eastwood, MM and Bar. There are also four of the 5/Border (97 Brigade) and Second Lieutenant Charles Case of the 11/Manchester and 20 Squadron RFC. Case, from Widness, was the observer in a Bristol Fighter piloted by Second Lieutenant N.Boulton. Their aircraft was shot down on 29 September 1918 near Montbrehain, probably be *Offizierstellvertreter* Frederick Altemeier of *Jasta 24*. They were Altemeier's eighteenth of his eventual twenty-one kills.

Vadencourt British Cemetery

Darkened by woods within the chateau grounds to its south, the cemetery was used from August 1917 until March and then again in October and November when the 5th, 47th and 61st CCS were at Bihécourt. All three units had begun work on 2 October and IX Corps Main Dressing Station was established at Vadencourt at the same time. There was a good deal of post-armistice concentration, including 36 men, largely of the 59th Division, who were brought in from the now disappeared Vendelles Churchyard and 15 from Vadencourt Chateau Cemetery. Today there are fewer than 800 remains. There are numbers of British, Indian and Canadian cavalry and many Sherwood Foresters who were killed in their abortive attack against Le Verguier. The fallen of March are represented by many men of the 1/8th Argyll & Sutherland Highlanders, 1/Northants and 3/RB. In plot III, row A, lie nearly a dozen soldiers, particularly of the 2/Sussex, killed in a railway accident in October 1918.

Among the fallen officers are Second Lieutenant Charles Blunt of 3/RB, a commissioned ranker (V.E.4), Lieutenant-Colonel J.H.Dimmer VC, MC (II.B.46) and Brigadier-General Sir William Kay, 6th Bart CMG, DSO, who, like Dimmer, was of the KRRC. (III.B.4) Kay, who had received six mentions in dispatches, was killed on 4 October while commanding 3 Brigade. Many of his brigade lie near him, as do a few Pioneers of the 1/Monmouth killed on the same day.

Vadencourt is a good example of a concentration cemetery. Roughly one third are unknown and headstones in the same row can show a variety of dates ranging from April 1917 to October 1918.

Vermand Communal Cemetery
This large communal cemetery, reached at the end of a gravel road on the west side of the town, contains the graves of five French soldiers, each with an unusual concrete cross. They are found near the war memorial at the northern end where there is another memorial to soldiers killed defending Vermand on 18 January 1871. Two British plots at either end of the cemetery are divided by the grave of Lance-Corporal Draper of the Berkshire Regiment. The southern plot has nine of Draper's comrades and two from the Gloucester Regiment of April 1917. There are others of the 61st Division from the same period in the northern plot, although most are from 1918. Four are men who died on 21 March, the remainder are a mixture of RGA, RE and infantry from September.

Villeret Churchyard Cemetery
Villeret Churchyard Cemetery is really the village communal cemetery. It is an open and bare collection of French and 18

This memorial on the N29, west of Vermand, commemorates ten young men and women of nearby Vraignes who were shot by the Nazis in August 1944.

British graves. Two men of the 10/Lincoln were buried in September 1917, while Private Sligo of the 1/Somerset Light Infantry died of wounds during the

Retreat. Most of the remainder are Manchester Terriers of the 66th Division. They include Captain Henry Leater of the 2/9th Battalion.

Vraignes Communal Cemetery
On the D34 south of Hancourt, this cemetery has eight British graves. Five are those of gunners killed in September 1918.

BIBLIOGRAPHY

C.Atkinson, *The Queen's Own Royal West Kent*, (London, 1929)

C.Bean, *Official History of Australia in the Great War*, (Sydney, 1943)

J.Boraston & C.Bax, *The Eighth Division in the War, 1914-1918*, (Medici, 1926)

H.Davson, *The History of the 35th Division in the Great War*, (Sifton, 1926)

L.de Grave, *The War History of the 5th Sherwood Foresters 1914-1918*.

C.Falls, *The Life of a Regiment (The History of the Gordon Highlanders)*, (Aberdeen, 1958)

A.Horne, *The Diary of a World War 1 Cavalry Officer*, (IWM Dept. of Documents)

L.Lumley, *The Eleventh Hussars*, (RUSI, 1936)

J.Lunt, *The Scarlet Lancers*, (Leo Cooper, 1993)

T.Marden, *A Short History of the 6th Division*, (Rees, 1920)

W.Meakin, *The 5th North Staffordshire & The North Midland Territorials 1914-1919*.

M.Middlebrook, *The Kaiser's Battle*, (Penguin, 1983)

P.Oldham, *The Hindenburg Line*, (Leo Cooper, 1997)

F.Petre, *The Royal Berkshire Regiment, Vol.2*

F.Petre, *The History of the Norfolk Regiment, Vol.2*

C.Potter & A.Fothergill, *The History of the the 2/6th Lancashire Fusiliers, (1927)*

H.Powell & J.Edwards, *The Sussex Yeomanry & 16th Bn, Royal Sussex Regiment*, (Melrose, 1921)

R.Priestley, *Breaking the Hindenburg Line*, (London, 1919)

P.Scott, *Dishonoured*, (Tom Donovan, 1994)

J.Shakespear, *The Thirty-Fourth Division*, (Witherby, 1921)

H.Stacke, *The Worcester Regiment in the Great War*, (Cheshire & Sons, 1929)

C.Ward, *The 74th (Yeomanry) Division in Syria and France*, (John Murray, 1922)

W.Weetman, *The 1/8th Sherwood Foresters in the Great War*.

P.Wright, *The First Buckinghamshire Battalion*, (Hazell, 1920)

F.Whitmore, *The 10th PWO Royal Hussars & Essex Yeomanry*, (Benham, 1920)

E.Wyrall, *The Gloucester Regiment in the War*, (Methuen, 1931)

The 59th Division, 1915-1918. Various authors, (Chesterfield, 1928)

The Official History of the Great War, France and Belgium. Various authors, (HMSO)

The War History of the 6th South Staffordshire. Various authors.

A History of the 8th Q.O.Royal West Kent. Various authors, (Privately printed, 1921)

140

SELECTIVE INDEX